T0366091

THE 100

CLARK D STUART

Order this book online at www.trafford.com
or email orders@trafford.com

Most Trafford titles are also available at major online book retailers.

Printed in the United States of America.

ISBN: 978-1-4669-1363-9 (sc)
ISBN: 978-1-4669-1362-2 (hc)
ISBN: 978-1-4669-1364-6 (e)

Library of Congress Control Number: 2012902318

Trafford rev. 04/27/2012

www.trafford.com

North America & international
toll-free: 1 888 232 4444 (USA & Canada)
phone: 250 383 6864 • fax: 812 355 4082

This book is dedicated with love,
respect and appreciation
to my friend,
Dr. Glenn Pfau.

FOREWORD

For the last 10 years of my life I have been blessed to be mentored by a great man. He has gone by many names and many titles over the years and he wears them all honorably. Some call him by the more formal titles of teacher, professor, doctor, mentor, trainer, or coach; others refer to him with less conventional titles such as guru, life coach, motivator, inspirer, or miracle man. Although all of these describe him well, I have been fortunate to be able to call him by the simpler title of friend.

During the time that I have known Dr. Glenn Pfau, I have heard his stories, learned his lessons and memorized his principles. These were not always new or profound and often I had heard them before, but they were always timely and when put together they became a powerful force in my life that enabled me to begin the process of becoming the man that I wanted to be.

Over the years, Dr. Pfau has worked with tens of thousands of people, helping them to change their lives for the better. He does not always tell us what we want to hear, nor does what he tells us always make us feel good about ourselves, but he does tell us what we need to hear and therein is the greatness of his teaching.

Many people will never have an opportunity to meet Dr. Pfau in person and to see his life for the miracle it is. It is for this reason that I chose to write this book, so that anyone who can read or hear these words will have the benefit of the simple lessons and the wisdom that often go unnoticed or get lost in the daily hustle and bustle of our over-stimulated lives. My hope, or dare I say, my prayer is that the principles in this book will touch you in a way that will help you to see and experience the miracles that are all around us every day.

I did not embark upon this project because of some tragic or catastrophic event that occurred in my life. The impacts of these lessons in my life are a subtle, constant pressure that over time changed me. By the time I retired from the military, I had decided that I was going to use these same principles that had so dramatically changed my life to help others. I do not have a hard-luck story for you. I grew up with both of my parents in a loving environment, in what would be considered an upper-income family. I was never abused, although I probably should have been punished for some of the stunts that I pulled as a kid and young adult. I never spent time in jail except for a short stint that I pulled as a deputy sheriff prior to joining the navy.

Except for the fact that I was a horrific student who got such poor grades that I barely passed high school, I can honestly say that I was perfectly average in every way and was destined for a life of perfect mediocrity in my youth. I had a lot of dreams but I lacked the discipline and focus to be able to accomplish much of anything without someone standing on my back and driving me, so when I announced that I wanted to be a Navy SEAL it came as a shock and surprise to anyone who knew me. Since I had never shown physical prowess of any sort nor had I ever gone about the business of setting any goals in my life up until this point, there was no particular reason that anyone should have expected me to be able to accomplish such a lofty goal. But accomplish it I did! After completing navy basic training I went to Basic Underwater Demolition School or (BUDS). Over the next six months this not-very-focused, not-very-disciplined, not-very-physical young man was transformed into a member of the U.S. Navy's elite special operations force, SEALs (SEa, Air, Land).

For the next 24 years I lived a life that many people could only imagine in their wildest dreams, traveling all over the world, jumping out of airplanes, diving out of submarines, shooting exotic weapons of all sorts, training foreign forces and assisting nations in trouble. I had an opportunity to serve with some of the finest men America has to offer. Living with these men who day in and day out are constantly striving to improve themselves in every way can change how one views the rest of the world. I have seen men accomplish spectacular feats that everyone said couldn't be done and overcome obstacles that were dubbed by many to be insurmountable to the point where I just came to expect these men to do the impossible as though it were an everyday occurrence.

Serving with such men changes a person and his perspective of reality. "Normal" becomes an entirely different standard and the high incidence in which I witnessed "impossible" feats over the years began to numb me to the miracles that I was observing. Being in the midst of this constant striving for improvement, I became accustomed to the pain, hard work, suffering, sacrifice and setbacks that come as part of the package of success. Over time, I began to take success for granted, missing the little struggles and little miracles that contribute to the greatness of the events that were happening around me every day.

And so it was when I met Dr. Pfau. He helped me to see the greatness in everyone and the miracles that are all around us every day. These miracles may not be record-breaking but in the struggles of everyday life, they represent breakthroughs and milestones that should be recognized and celebrated. This book is a testament to the struggles that we all face every day in our lives that we must rise up to and overcome in order to be our best and to achieve the miracle that we want to see. These principles that Dr. Pfau taught me have made a profound difference in many peoples' lives and they can be the foundation for change in your life as well.

Be the miracle that you want to see.

Clark Stuart
May 2011

These principles are used as a part of my Executive Presentations Skills Training Course. Each has its own significance and each is able to stand alone. Although they are numbered for reference purposes, they are not presented in any particular order of importance. There are far more than 100 principles of communications but these are the most common and like all great principles, they have a timeless quality making them just as meaningful today as they were in the beginning of time and ensuring that they will maintain their significance far into the future. And so, I now present to you *The 100.*

THE 100

1. Knowledge is power. If I knew better, I would do better.
2. We do not determine our future; we determine our habits, and our habits determine our future.
3. Audiences have a limited capacity to absorb information.
4. All work in life falls into three basic categories: Leading, Selling or Teaching.
5. Audiences think very highly of themselves.
6. Things don't have credibility; people have credibility.
7. We must find our authentic selves.
8. The common outcome of communication is miscommunication.
9. The Three Vs of Communications
10. Practice makes permanent.
    Perfect practice make perfect.
11. Great speakers start where the audience is.
12. Reading a speech destroys 90% of its effectiveness.

13. There are only two inches between cowering and towering.
14. Great speakers are upbeat, confident, energetic and have a can-do spirit.
15. There are no dull topics, just dull speakers.
16. Confidence cannot be taught, it must be caught.
17. No profanity
18. Greatness is not a single event; it is the synergistic effect of thousands of tiny details coming together to become more than the sum of its parts.
19. Think in concepts, not words.
20. Look up, lock in, and speak to one person.
21. Begin and end with a smile.
22. You never get a second chance to make a first impression.
23. Do not look at notes for first or last 10 percent of a presentation.
24. Rule of Cards
25. Eye Contact
26. Life is a World Cup with no timeouts. You are ALWAYS on!
27. Remove all distracters from belts, pockets and body before speaking.
28. Hand gestures should support, reinforce and back up our words.

29. Start your day with an affirmation.
30. The Three Ps of Voice
31. Martin Luther King's Keys to an Effective Presentation
32. Do the thing you fear, and the thing you fear will disappear.
33. Until I try to do something that I have not already mastered, I will not grow.
34. Whatever the mind can conceive and the heart can believe, the body can achieve.
35. Luck is when planning and preparation intersect opportunity.
36. Success leaves clues.
37. Avoid qualifiers.
38. It is ten times worse to look up than down.
39. Get out of the box.
40. We make a living by what we get; we make a life by what we give.
41. It is not a tragedy to die with dreams unfulfilled, but it is a tragedy to die without dreams.
42. Passion drives the message but there must be a unique balance between passion and substance.
43. I must become comfortable being uncomfortable.
44. 10—80—10 Rule of Presentation Development
45. Never write a presentation in advance.

46. Practice Allowed
47. As confidence grows, speaking rate slows.
48. To live without discipline is to die without dignity.
49. The quality of a person's life is in direct proportion to their commitment to excellence, regardless of their chosen field of endeavor.
50. Repeat words and phrases for emphasis.
51. There is nothing as powerful as a well-placed pause.
52. Share personal anecdotes.
53. Directionality With Flexibility
54. Use quotes.
55. Use alliterations.
56. Make the presentation sticky.
57. Give the audience a conclusion indicator.
58. Less than 10% of our nervousness transmits to the audience.
59. Our attitude, not our aptitude, determines our altitude.
60. Take Risks
61. Four Types of Presentations
62. Never turn your back on the audience.
63. Audiences love humor, especially self-deprecating humor.
64. To eliminate fillers, we must implement "STS".

65. If I talk to everyone, I will communicate with no one; if I talk to one person, I will communicate with everyone.
66. Rule of THREE
67. Call people out by name.
68. Don't tell the audience what you are going to do or say, just do or say it.
69. Aristotle's Three Components of Communications.
70. Do not ask the audience to pay attention; capture their attention.
71. I am in control.
72. Start slowly.
73. "The plan is nothing, but planning is everything."
74. We must learn to be where the puck is going, not where the puck is.
75. You miss every shot you don't take.
76. Courage is not the absence of fear; it is the ability to do what is right in the face of it.
77. We all suffer from self-doubt.
78. Failure is simply the learning process of success.
79. Three Parts of a Speech
80. Better a grand failure than a mediocre success.
81. The company we keep becomes a reflection of ourselves.

82. Successful people are not lucky; they are doing something right and doing it consistently.
83. If success was easy, everyone would have it.
84. Good is the enemy of excellence.
85. Great leaders take more responsibility than they should when things go wrong and less credit than they should when things go right.
86. No one cares how much I know until they know how much I care.
87. The best way to predict the future is to create it.
88. P = P–I
89. Audiences are very smart.
90. A leader is a person with a vision and the ability to articulate that vision so vividly and so powerfully that it becomes the vision of others.
91. Learn to put your hands at your side.
92. Discontent is the first step forward in the progress of a man.
93. Constantly challenge yourself to be the best every day.
94. You are only as good as your last game.
95. Paint word pictures.
96. Nothing succeeds like success.
97. Use an "X" Factor.
98. Successful people are willing to do what unsuccessful people are not willing to do.
99. Use Visual Aids.
100. Develop three to four stump speeches.

THE 100

1

KNOWLEDGE IS POWER. IF I KNEW BETTER, I WOULD DO BETTER.

Nobody wakes up in the morning and says to himself, "I want to be a loser today." People do not intentionally set out to do things wrong in life so that they will look bad. People who make wrong choices do not understand or recognize the impact their choices are going to have on their lives. What others see in us is a reflection of the choices that we make every day. These choices are dictated by a combination of our culture, our environment and our history. Even though people generally know what is right and what is wrong, they will choose to do the wrong thing because they believe the consequences of that action will be less onerous than the difficulty they will have to endure if they do the right thing. Human nature often moves us to take the path of least resistance, so we must resist the temptation to do what is natural and make a conscious choice to rise up to be better.

Animals do what is natural and it is our ability to make choices that make us human. By making poor choices we are creating two problems. One is that we may or may not get away with it and will have to face the consequences of our actions. When we make wrong or poor choices, others observe this and make judgments about us based on what they have observed and their opinions may impact our future.

Another problem we have created by our conscious decision to do the wrong thing is that it creates a slippery slope from which it is very difficult to recover. Making a poor choice and getting away with it makes the next poor choice that much easier. We make thousands of tiny decisions every day of our lives and if we start to make poor decisions, then we have a tendency to continue to make poor decisions based on that foundation. Eventually, that foundation will lead us to our own demise.

Integrity is doing what is right when we think that no one is watching. We have many choices to make every day of our lives. We need to make these choices based on the understanding of how our decisions impact our future. Knowledge is power. If I knew better, I would do better.

2

WE DO NOT DETERMINE OUR FUTURE; WE DETERMINE OUR HABITS, AND OUR HABITS DETERMINE OUR FUTURE.

Habits are the most misunderstood, neglected, abused and yet powerful forces in our lives. They are neutral entities, neither good nor bad, until we embrace them and yet are an absolute necessity for achieving success. Habits enable us to respond to situations quickly and accurately without having to go through the cumbersome process of thinking which slows us down. Imagine how difficult life would be if we had to consciously think about every action we took. Our lives would slow down tremendously and we would be subjected to many dangers that we otherwise instinctively avoid through the application of habit.

Like any tool that we have in our kit, a habit can be good or bad depending on how it is used and the situation in which it must be applied. Take, for example, a person who trains himself to move slowly and methodically to ensure an error-free process. This is great if there is never any need to speed up, but what happens when a situation demands speed as well as accuracy? In this case, the habitual, slow and methodical process is a disadvantage.

We should never underestimate the impact of our habits because they are the single most powerful determining factor of success or failure. Habits are so powerful that it is possible to observe and record them and use them as a predictor of someone's future behavior unless training is applied with sufficient emphasis to change the habit.

One of the problems with habits is that they are very subtle with their force, so subtle that while we may actually intend to do something that is contradictory to our habitual response, stress may evoke the habitual response. When we are put under stress because of time constraints, danger, self-consciousness, fatigue or anxiety, we will invariably resort to the one thing that does not require thought and that is our habits.

Because habits are such a powerful force in our lives we can never take them for granted. We need to constantly evaluate and reassess our actions to ensure that we are establishing and maintaining good habits that improve and enrich our lives.

3

AUDIENCES HAVE A LIMITED CAPACITY TO ABSORB NEW INFORMATION.

There are several reasons why speakers overload their audiences with information. One is when they are self-conscious about what the audience is going to think of them. This is natural. Unfortunately, the natural response to this fear is not necessarily the best response. Our natural response is to want to show the audience how smart we are and we tend to do this by providing the audience with more information than they need or can handle. Secondly, at the other end of the scale is the egomaniac who intentionally wants to show the audience how smart he is.

Overloading the audience with information will shut them down and turn them off to what you are trying to convey regardless or your objective. Information overload often occurs when speakers do not understand the limitations of their audience. Most people can only process about six new pieces of information if they are very interested in the topic. On the other hand, if the audience members are not interested in the topic, they will have trouble remembering even three.

The limited capacity of most people to retain statistical information makes it very important for us as speakers to not add more information than necessary to make our point. One way to help an audience remember is to make associations to known and understood patterns of information. People have a near infinite capacity to remember patterns. Applying your new information to an existing pattern helps to reduce the amount of new information that an audience must process.

Always remember that it is the responsibility of the speaker to determine what information the audience needs to remember. Therefore, it is also the responsibility of the speaker to put information into a format that is easy to remember. Too many speakers throw a garbage can of information at an audience and then just hope they get what they need. Generally, in these circumstances, the audience does not get anything significant out of the presentation. They tire of trying to weed through the material that does not apply to them to determine what is important. Eventually they may give up in frustration. Since audiences have a limited capacity to absorb new information, speakers need to have a good strategy to ensure that their audience get what they need and what they will find most useful.

#4

ALL WORK IN LIFE FALLS INTO THREE BASIC CATEGORIES: LEADING, SELLING OR TEACHING.

Our life is a combination of Leading, Selling or Teaching and usually our life's work has an emphasis in one of these disciplines. As different as each of these categories may seem, they all have one very common element. They are all about the art of influencing others. As leaders, we are constantly influencing our people toward our organization's goal or the vision we have of our company's purpose. Salespersons are constantly trying to influence people toward recognizing the value of a product so that they will purchase it. Teachers are constantly influencing our students to recognize the importance of the information that is being presented to them so that they will learn.

Each of these disciplines has a very rigid formal meaning, but the skills involved play an important informal role in our everyday lives as well. For example, we must lead within our family life or at our workplace, sell ourselves or teach others by example. Whether you label yourself a leader, a salesperson, or a teacher, you are in the business of influencing others and the primary way to do this is through communications.

In order to be an effective influencer, you must communicate; how well you communicate will determine how well you perform as a leader, a salesperson or a teacher. Once we recognize that communication is the primary means of influencing others then we understand that this is where we must focus our training effort.

Communication is often neglected and taken for granted because it is viewed as a rudimentary skill that everyone brings to the table. Many believe that some people are just natural or lucky because they are good communicators. Nothing can be further from the truth. We develop our communication habits over time. The key is to know which of these habits are good and which ones are bad and how to make the necessary changes to improve our communication skills.

The truth is that every good communicator probably was once a poor communicator who learned how to become better. It is never too late to start training to improve your skills as a communicator. All you need is a desire and the willingness to risk talking to people whom you respect and listening to what they have to say. Our future is not set unless and until we refuse to change. We make our own choices about setting our lives on a fixed course to the final destination we want to reach.

5

AUDIENCES THINK VERY HIGHLY OF THEMSELVES.

As an influencer, you want to be constantly aware that audiences think very highly of themselves. Even prior to your appearance before them, they are making a determination about whether or not you are a person they are going to allow to influence them. When audiences are asked to rate themselves in various areas of their lives, they are always going to rate themselves "high." Almost no one will rate himself or herself below average in any given category unless he or she has a very poor self-image. A professional influencer must understand how those in the audience see themselves because this is going to influence how they respond to the presenter.

Many communicators think that they will connect with their audience if they come in at their level, by trying to mirror them by dressing like them or talking like them and using the same lingo or slang. This tactic may have a place in the development of relationships in which a person has a long time to establish and develop a pattern of influence; however, this is not the case for speakers or influencers attempting to communicate a specific message. Most leaders, salespersons and teachers have only small windows to work within to establish their influence. If the audience sees the presenter as too much like themselves, then that speaker loses an influential edge. Audiences are looking for indicators of knowledge, skills and abilities beyond their own in the speaker.

While audiences think very highly of themselves and will not rate themselves below the 50th percentile, anyone's ability can be measured on a bell curve and 50 percent of the audience will be below average in any given category of evaluation. If we, as speakers, base our actions on the reality of the audience, we run the risk of being rated well below their own perception of themselves and thus losing the influential edge.

We must also keep in mind that it is not in the interest of the communicator to help the audience to understand the truth about themselves. We need to accept that audiences think very highly about themselves and we want to build on that vision that they have of themselves. If we do anything that is contrary to the pre-developed vision those in the audience have of themselves, we will lose credibility and thus the ability to influence the audience. Don't let the reality of the audience fool you. Audiences think very highly of themselves.

#6

THINGS DON'T HAVE CREDIBILITY; PEOPLE HAVE CREDIBILITY.

One of the common conditions of public speaking is fear and anxiety. Because of this, many speakers have a tendency to take the focus off themselves and put it on something else. They try to find a way to do the presentation without actually being present themselves. At the extreme are speakers who present slide shows while they stand in the dark, in the back of a class, and talk to the slides they are projecting onto a screen. Like the Wizard of Oz who tells Dorothy to pay no attention to the man behind the curtain, this kind of speaker wants to be a faceless, anonymous voice that simply puts out information.

Then, there are those speakers who read their presentations or hide behind podiums in an attempt to place barriers between themselves and the audience. Remember that audiences are looking to the speaker to determine if the information that is being presented to them has any credibility or will influence them at all. If the speaker makes the audience feel good and convinces them that he is a credible individual, then everything he says will be perceived as credible. On the other hand, if the speaker does not succeed in making the audience feel good or in convincing them that he has credibility, then the audience will not believe anything the speaker says regardless of its legitimacy.

There have been many great speakers throughout history who have sold absolute garbage to entire nations of people simply by understanding this principle. Good speakers understand that they must first sell themselves to the audience. Once they have done this, then they can begin to provide supporting evidence. If, however, the speaker tries to sell information first, before selling himself, then his effectiveness as an influencer will diminish to the point where it might have been better to send out an email or a flyer with the necessary information.

Never underestimate your own value in the delivery of a presentation. The presenter gives the information credibility, not the other way around.

7

WE MUST FIND OUR AUTHENTIC SELVES.

Although we may not think of ourselves as disingenuous, we are, however, aggregates of all our life experiences and therein lies the problem. We tend to adapt our behavior according to the experiences we have in life so that, over time, we become a network of accumulated habitual responses to stimuli of good and bad experiences. Eventually, our resulting behavior involves a series of defense mechanisms designed to protect us from the emotional strain of bad experiences.

Public speaking produces a lot of deep emotions in people. It is the number one phobia in the United States, feared more than death itself. Because public speaking is so feared, many speakers develop defense mechanisms to protect their basic identities from the possible negative judgments of their audience. They do this because they do not want their true persona to be affected by a possible poor performance and/or the perceived disapproval of the audience.

Many people simply avoid public speaking entirely as a way of protecting themselves; others make changes in their normal behavior to the point where they are barely recognized as the same person when they ascend to the stage. A common defense mechanism includes putting objects such as podiums or tables between the speaker and the audience. Other measures include taking a closed body posture, not looking directly at the audience but over their heads, not moving or being very rigid, not using hand gestures, using fillers to avoid silence or rambling in a monotone. All of these behaviors are designed to protect the speaker from exposing himself to an audience.

Some speakers have been using protective behaviors like these for so long that their actions have become habitual and they do not even know who their authentic self is anymore. In an attempt to protect our authentic self, we may have developed habits that keep us from recognizing the greatness within ourselves. It is not until we take a chance and begin to strip away those protective habits that we begin to see who we really are and accept who we were meant to be.

Audiences can see when a speaker is not genuine and authentic. If they fail to perceive a presenter as authentic, they may assume he is hiding something and thus loses the power to influence them. As speakers, we must find and embrace our authentic self before we can begin to realize our potential to influence others.

8

THE COMMON OUTCOME OF COMMUNICATION IS MISCOMMUNICATION.

It is very seldom that any of us take a serious look at our own communications process. After all, why should we? We have been communicating one way or another since we were born and for most of us it seems to have worked well enough thus far. Consequently, few of us see the need to assess and evaluate and amend our communications process.

The truth is that communications is a very complicated process that we pretty much take for granted. We just assume that what we say is what is being heard by others but this may not be the case.

At the start of the communications process, the transmitter has an idea that he enters into an encoding process that formulates how he is going to transmit the information to the receiver. The encoder takes all of the information that the transmitter has accumulated over a lifetime from his family, culture, education, trial and error, perspective, values and beliefs and puts it into a format that he believes will communicate the intent of the message. This encoding process includes the hand gestures, facial expressions, vocal pitch, power and pace, language, word choice, organization, body posture, time, place, context, preparation, situation and supporting material. All of these factors will be coordinated by the transmitter to produce the most influential impact and sent to the receiver.

Then, the receiver enters the message into his own decoder and evaluates the hand gestures, facial gestures, vocal pitch, power and pace, language, word choice, organization, body posture, time, place, context, preparation, situation and supporting material through layers of a decoding system developed over a lifetime of experiences. This includes processing all of the transmitted data through the filter of the receiver's culture, education, trial and error, perspective, values and beliefs.

When we consider the process of communications in this context, it is amazing that we are able to communicate with each other at all. It is also much easier to understand how a speaker can miscommunicate a message to an audience. To add to the problem, most of us are not accustomed to communicating cross-culturally and therefore often do not understand the nuances that exist when people from different cultural backgrounds attempt to communicate with each other. The communications process is difficult enough between people from the same culture. Anyone who has walked the aisle of a bookstore and perused the shelves of the "relationship section" will see that the majority of helpful offerings involve communications between men and women of the same culture.

It does not matter what you say in a conversation, it only matters what the receiver hears and decodes. Our intentions count for much less.

9

THE THREE Vs OF COMMUNICATIONS

Communications can be broken down into three primary components: Verbal, Vocal, and Visual. Each one of these is an essential part of the communications process. Most people put a very high emphasis on the verbal part of communications, the words that are used to communicate. Research, however, has proven that it is not what you say but how you say it that counts. Words have emotional meaning based on the vocal element or how they are said and the visual component or body language that the speaker uses to support his words. The audience is constantly looking to the speaker to provide the context of the words being spoken. In this light, the speaker is the contextual framer of the message being communicated.

Audiences take in 75 percent of their information visually and only 13 percent through hearing and yet many speakers seem to do everything in their power to eliminate the visual element of communications by becoming as invisible as possible to their audience in order to limit their emotional exposure to the unknown. This is why it is so important to be willing to accept risk in order to be effective. If, as in the case of radio announcements or telephone sales, the visual element is removed from the communications process then the vocal element takes on an even greater significance. The following is the percentage breakout of the three "Vs" of communications based on how much of the message is transmitted by each:

Verbal	(words)	7%
Vocal	(voice inflection)	38%
Visual	(body language)	55%

The following is a percentage breakout of the parts of communications based on how much of the message is transmitted by each with the visual element removed:

Verbal	(words)	16%
Vocal	(voice inflection)	84%

This information should be helpful to speakers who are putting together a presentation. Often we spend 99 percent of our time determining the words that we are going to use in a presentation and fail to plan the vocal and visual impressions we want to convey.

10

PRACTICE MAKES ~~PERFECT.~~ Permanent

PERFECT PRACTICE MAKES PERFECT.

This is probably one of the most misquoted principles out there. 'Practice makes perfect` sounds good but is a little too simple a phrase for those aspiring to world-class performance in their chosen endeavors. The act of doing something over and over again incorrectly only ensures that we get really good at doing something wrong! It is not enough in life to do something over and over again with the hope that by doing it repeatedly, we will eventually perform the action perfectly.

It is true that continual and repeated practice will develop habits that become hard to break later. Practicing the performance of any skill incorrectly will result in the development of bad habits that make it very difficult to improve performance. In this case, practice does not make perfect but may make an incorrect action permanent. The legendary football coach Vince Lombardi knew this and he was fanatical about how his team practiced. It was not enough just to show up and go through the motions on a daily basis hoping to get better. Lombardi was a stickler for detail and was constantly focused on the small things that when put together would synergize the efforts of the team and propel them toward victory.

If we truly desire high levels of performance in any skill, we must practice; however, we must practice with a constant focus on making the changes needed to improve performance. In this way, we perfect our practice and develop good habits that will lead to world-class performance. Perfect practice makes perfect.

11

GREAT SPEAKERS START WHERE THE AUDIENCE IS.

Because we are often self-conscious when we must stand up before an audience, many speakers are more concerned about what is important to them rather than what is important to the audience. One element that all great speakers have is a good understanding of their audience and the needs of that audience. Once a speaker has conducted a thorough assessment of the audience, then he is ready to prepare and present a program that is designed specifically for that audience. This is what makes for great presentations. Being able to put the information of a presentation into a context that is specifically designed for that audience is one of the elements that can turn an average speaker into a great speaker.

Every audience is special and unique. The more the speaker understands this, the better he will be able to focus his presentation to that particular audience. To achieve this, it is essential for a presenter to examine the characteristics of each audience he will be addressing. The following includes some of these characteristics:

Hobbies	Interest	Commonalities
Age	Sex	Culture
Education	Backgrounds	Organization
Affiliations	Location	Race
Religion	History	Shared Experiences
Common Goals	Positions	Morals
Intergroup Relationships	Group Dynamic	Abilities
Economic Status	Jobs	Skills
Social Status	Likes	Desires
Ambitions	Values	

Although this is not an all-inclusive list, these are some of the things a speaker should take into consideration when preparing to stand up before an audience. Every speaker should ask: who are these people waiting to hear what I have to say? He should do everything possible to understand as much as possible about the audience as he prepares his presentation. A great presentation is about the audience and not about the speaker or his ego. This is sometimes easy for a speaker to forget after he has a few successes under his belt. Successful presenters will remember that true greatness comes from the audiences and this can only be gained by understanding their audiences and acknowledging what is important to them. By doing so, a speaker will be able to prepare a presentation that is specifically tailored and suited to his audience. This will make an audience feel special and unique and they will appreciate the fact that the speaker took the time to recognize their uniqueness.

Always start with the audience!

12

READING A SPEECH DESTROYS 90% OF ITS EFFECTIVENESS.

Some of my favorite communications jokes involve people reading speeches. One of them is a cartoon that shows a picture of a man standing behind a podium as the audience is throwing things at him. The man sitting in the chair next to him calmly states, "It's a great speech, you're just reading it poorly." Another has an antic offering this feedback: There were only three things wrong with your speech; 1) You read it. 2) You read it poorly. 3) You didn't say anything worth listening to.

Dale Carnegie said that if you read a speech, you destroy 90 percent of its effectiveness. Why is this? Why are audiences so unresponsive to people who read speeches to them? The very action of reading to an audience makes many statements that can be adversely interpreted by the audience. First, reading a presentation to an audience makes a statement that the words are not coming from the heart. If the message was sincere, the speaker would not have had to read it.

Second, by reading his speech, the presenter is telling the audience that what he is saying is not important enough for him to learn so that he would not have to read it.

Third, a "reader" is telling the audience that he doesn't trust them enough to read his message for themselves so he feels it necessary to take the time to read it to them aloud.

Reading a speech is a way to insult an audience in a very direct manner. Remember that the audience is looking to the speaker to provide the contextual framework for the information they are receiving. If we read a presentation, we are stating that the information is not important, that it is not reflective of the presenter, and that the audience is too dumb or untrustworthy to read it for themselves. Reading does provide a context with which to interpret the presentation, but it is certainly not a good context.

Reading a speech does have an appropriate place and time but it should be used sparingly and with a specific purpose that should be explained to the audience. For example:

— If it is new material and the speaker has not been able to review it adequately.
— When paraphrasing would detract from the significance of the actual wording.
— When a presenter is delivering a written prepared speech for a speaker in absentia.
— When providing information that is specific such as numbers or names that must be delivered accurately.
— When delivering an extensive quote that must be delivered as written or spoken.

Above all, if it is necessary to read some material, it is best to avoid doing so during the opening or conclusion of a presentation. These are the points where a speaker wants all of his communications to be coming directly from the heart. Reading the material will significantly detract from this.

13

THERE ARE ONLY TWO INCHES BETWEEN COWERING AND TOWERING.

It is the subtleties in life that make the essential difference between success and failure. Without the help of trained professionals, it is difficult to train ourselves to evaluate the perceptions of our audience. Audiences are looking to every detail and nuance of our presence as they develop the context within which they will interpret our message. Our physical appearance is one of those elements that audiences will scrutinize very closely and assess carefully. Before we utter a word, our posture sends a very important message. Even slight variations in our posture project messages to our audience. Lowering the head, a slight slumping or rounding of the shoulders, sticking the chin out, rounding our back, failure to stand upright, tightening the stomach muscles are all posture variations noticeable to the audience.

Good posture projects confidence without a word being spoken. This projection of confidence speaks volumes to an audience as they prepare to hear what a speaker has to say. Good posture tells the audience that I have something to say that is important to you and I believe in it. By contrast, poor posture speaks volumes as well. Poor posture says that I lack discipline and am totally unaware or uncaring of the image that I project. Poor posture tells the audience that a speaker is not confident in what he has to say nor is he sure that they need or want to hear it.

All of this is interpreted on a conscious level by people who are very aware and on a subconscious level by those who may be less aware of those environmental factors that impact their feelings. The audience may not even know why they don't like the speaker or don't believe in what he is saying. That is the power of the subconscious mind. Our minds are so powerful that we are interpreting things all the time on a subconscious level that we are not even aware of consciously. Our subconscious is constantly providing input that is helping us to provide context for and assisting us to interpret the world around us.

Many of us have been told our entire lives that we need to stand up straight, stick our chests out, pull our chins in and to suck in our guts. We know what looks good and people are positively influenced by things that they think look good or things that they like. On the other hand, we are generally influenced negatively by things that we don't like. For this reason it is important as communicators to be aware of how we look to others and to insure that we train ourselves to develop and maintain good posture.

14

GREAT SPEAKERS ARE UPBEAT, CONFIDENT, ENERGETIC AND HAVE A CAN-DO SPIRIT.

Because a presenter is the contextual framer of his speaking environment, he sets the tone for everything that follows. Audiences look to the speaker to determine how they should feel and what they should expect. If he wants an audience to be drowsy, disinterested and listless all a speaker has to do is come across as lifeless to his audience. There are plenty of people going through life in a daze and they certainly do not need any help being drowsy, disinterested and listless. People will pay attention to things that interest them and so for a speaker to gain the attention of an audience, he must appear interesting. This may be counterintuitive to inexperienced public speakers because their instinct is to try to shrink away from the audience and not reveal themselves.

Trying to move the attention away from themselves and focus it on the topic of the presentation is a trap that would-be professional speakers fall into in an attempt to avoid revealing any personal emotion to the audience. To do this is to lose the power to generate emotion in an audience. A recitation of statistics does not move an audience to action; audiences are moved to action by their emotions. If we are unable to generate those emotions, we will never be effective in influencing our audience to action of any sort.

As speakers, we must express the emotion we want to generate in our audience. We remember speakers who are upbeat and energetic. These are indicators of happiness and success in life. When we meet people who project the emotions associated with these traits, we become interested so that we can learn their secret. Nothing succeeds like success and we all want to be successful. When we find people who project the emotions associated with happiness and success, we instinctively want to work with them. No one wants to take advice from or work with people who are having troubles or are having a hard time making things work. Everyone wants to work with people and do business with people who are successful. That is why successful businessmen in any field of endeavor will always maintain a positive attitude and demeanor in public regardless of what difficulties they are facing in their lives. We must be the emotion that we want to see in our audience. Never be afraid to show emotion and to be upbeat, confident and energetic for your audience.

15

THERE ARE NO DULL TOPICS, JUST DULL SPEAKERS.

Successful communications are based on the relationship that a presenter develops with an audience. That relationship begins to develop even before an audience ever sees the speaker and is based on the environment, conditions and surroundings of the venue where the meeting is going to take place. As an example, if the audience is a class and the meeting is taking place in a classroom then just by the very nature of that situation, the speaker is perceived as a teacher. The audience already has a certain expectation of what to expect from that speaker. Added to this is any research the audience has done or hearsay they may have received about the speaker prior to his arrival.

This is why great communicators control as many of these factors as possible, but controlling expectations can be difficult. The reputation that any of us brings with us begins to make an impact on how an audience will view our topic even prior to our arrival on the stage. From a speaker's perspective a topic may be easier or more difficult to talk about based on the complexity of the speaker's personal interest in the subject.

If a presenter is a poor speaker, he may try to shift the blame of a boring presentation onto the topic. When an audience identifies the topic as being boring, it is generally because the speaker has placed all of the focus on the topic to account for a poor delivery. What all speakers must understand is that it is impossible to separate the topic from the speaker. The speaker becomes the representative of the topic.

We very rarely hear anyone say of a presentation that the topic was really boring, but the speaker was great. The topic and presenter are evaluated as one and being boring is one of the worst things a speaker can ever be accused of. An audience is far more interested in the relationship that the speaker develops with them than the topic that is being presented. If a speaker is interesting, the topic will seem interesting by association; if the speaker is boring and uninteresting, then anything he talks about will seem the same.

As communicators, we have the ability to bring topics to life with the energy and passion that we add to them through our personalities. The only way to do this is to share a piece of our authentic selves with the audience.

16

CONFIDENCE CANNOT BE TAUGHT, IT MUST BE CAUGHT.

If anyone ever tries to tell you that they want to teach you how to be self-confident, run away as fast as you can. This would be like someone saying they were going to teach you joy or peace or love. Confidence is not something that is learned like math or history. It is not a thing made up of specific facts, details and statistics. Self-confidence is a feeling that one has about himself and such feelings cannot be taught. How a person feels about himself is a result of all of the positive or negative input and the presence or absence of positive reinforcement he has received throughout all the years of his life.

Over time, we build barriers that are designed to protect us from the input of others into our lives. These barriers keep people from seeing who we really are so that we do not expose ourselves to their perceptions about us. In order to gain confidence, we must see ourselves as we really are after we strip away all the protective barriers that we have built between ourselves and our audience. This is the authentic self referred to earlier and this is who the audience is looking for in the speaker standing before them.

Personal development is one of the most challenging journeys that a person can embark on. It is a very difficult process and requires an amazing amount of discipline. To look at ourselves honestly and accept criticism and consider recommendations from others on how to change ourselves to be more effective is a process that leaves us feeling very exposed and vulnerable. Once we do this, however, and we begin to see ourselves succeed, we cannot help but welcome change, change for the better that will lead us to the success we desire. Again, nothing succeeds like success and each success we achieve leads us to believe in ourselves. This feeling of belief in what we are doing translates into a feeling of confidence in the actions and decisions we are making that have led to success.

No one can teach you confidence and no one can give it to you. Confidence is something that each one of us has to go out and get for ourselves. There are people who can help set up an environment that will enhance our ability to succeed, but success must be earned by each of us through hard-fought efforts and life experiences. Confidence is a gift that one can only receive from oneself. It comes with taking chances and learning to become as comfortable with losing as with winning. The key is to learn from the losses so that you can grow and build on your success to become more self-confident.

17

NO PROFANITY

Profanity is a very dangerous tool to have in the toolbox of communication options. It has many sharp edges and it can inflict untold damage if you chose to wield it. Profanity has all the precision of a grenade; when it goes off it makes a mess of everything.

Profanity works against us in three primary ways. First, profanity is normally a developed habit based on the culture that we are a part of. In many cultures, it is a part of everyday language. This habitual use of profanity leads to an entirely new set of problems outside of that culture. Profanity can become such a part of a person's natural pattern of speech that he may not even realize he is using it at inappropriate times.

The second problem associated with the use of profanity is how it is perceived by an audience. A speaker may think he is using profanity as an explanative or to add emphasis to a point. The problem is that many people interpret the use of profanity as a speaker's lack of ability to find the proper words to express the ideas he wants to communicate. This can translate into the speaker being perceived as illiterate or even uneducated and, to put it bluntly, just not very smart. These are not generally things that work to any speaker's advantage as he attempts to influence an audience.

The third problem with using profanity is that it is abrasive and insulting to many people. This is especially true with audiences who don't know us and with whom we must be concerned about how we make them feel. For many, the use of profanity feels like a personal affront even though that is not how it is intended by the speaker. Many people use profanity thinking that it is in no way related to the audience, but there are many people who are not accustomed to hearing it and they can easily misinterpret a speaker's message.

Because profanity is so dangerous, I would encourage you to do an assessment of your pattern of speech and if you use profanity, stop. There are few things that will do more harm to your image than using profanity. For this reason, it is best to eliminate the use of it in every area of your life. This is the only way to ensure that it does not slip out as part of a habitual response to stress.

18

GREATNESS
IS NOT A SINGLE EVENT;
IT IS THE SYNERGISTIC
EFFECT OF THOUSANDS
OF TINY DETAILS COMING
TOGETHER TO BECOME
MORE THAN THE SUM
OF ITS PARTS.

As we observe people who are successful, we only see the end product of a great deal of hard work. We may make a determination that this is where we want to be without having seen the many years of struggle, sacrifice, discipline, focus, pain, and failure that the successful person had to deal with to achieve that desired end state. We do not see the long series of choices that this person had to make along the way. This is one of those important life realizations that we need to come to terms with or we will always be looking in the wrong place for success.

When we see people who have achieved success at any endeavor, we are simply seeing a culmination of a series of events and choices that have led these people to that crowning moment of victory or success in their lives. Success and failure are not singular events in anyone's life. They are the results of a series of small choices that have led ultimately to that defining moment where the success or failure will be recognized. These choices are choices we make every day of our lives. To recognize that we all have the same amount of time in our lives empowers us to take control of our life through our own choices of what to do with that time.

Success and failure are neutral characters in the scheme of life. They are neither friend nor foe. They are out there all the time, waiting for each of us to make a choice about what we are going to do with our time. The thousands of tiny choices that we make every day will lead us toward success or toward failure depending on the quality of our choices.

We can help ourselves to move more quickly toward our goal by developing good daily habits that will allow us to make the best choice in any situation without having to think about it. Our nature is to always take the easy way out if it is an option and that is why establishing a good habit can be so helpful. We simply make it a part of our habitual process to do what is right. This is why it is so important to make sure the habits that we develop are good habits because our habits will become the chains that will bind us to our future.

Should I get up or sleep in? Should I study or watch TV? Should I read a self-help book or a popular novel? Should I get something to eat or work out? Should I do my laundry or go to the beach? Should I write this book or play XBOX? Should I go back to school or go on a vacation?

What choices are you making today that will affect your success or failure in the future?

19

THINK IN CONCEPTS, NOT WORDS.

A lot of things happen to us physiologically when we are under stress. One major event is the injection of chemicals into our system that results in certain physiological responses. Our heart rate increases, our blood pressure rises, our muscles tighten, we experience a loss of fine motor skills, our vision narrows and above all we lose our ability to reason under stress. This is where we revert to our habitual responses as our fight-or-flight mechanism kicks into action.

Public speaking tends to induce stress and even the most experienced speakers develop a certain level of anxiety associated with standing up before an audience. Experienced speakers, however, have learned how to focus the energy generated by the adrenaline injection and use it to their advantage. As this excess energy builds up in our system we have a need to burn it off. We need to incorporate it into our presentation, developing exciting and dynamic speeches.

The inability to reason and the lack of cognitive focus present a specific problem for many people. Speakers under stress may stand up and forget what it was that they wanted to say. More precisely, they forget the words they wanted to use and because they do not remember the words, they don't know what to say.

Under pressure we may lose the ability to remember the exact verbiage that we wanted to use in our presentation. This does not mean that we lose the ability to speak; it simply means that we cannot remember the exact words so we end up saying nothing. If we attempt to recite a memorized speech, we often make mistakes. This is one of the reasons that I recommend never attempting to memorize a presentation. Rather than attempting to remember the exact words, I recommend breaking a presentation down into basic topic areas and making a note of the topics. Practice talking about each of the topics in a generalized manner, being less focused on the words and more focused on covering the general topic. In breaking a presentation down into general concepts, there is far less to remember and therefore much less to forget when we are under stress.

Remember, an audience has no idea what the speaker wants to say. So in giving a presentation, be forgiving of the things that you forget to say because the audience has no idea that you didn't say these things unless you project this information to them in some way. Focus on the basic concepts that you want to present and then just talk to them. This is how great speakers maintain their directionality with flexibility, through concepts and not words.

20

LOOK UP, LOCK IN, AND SPEAK TO ONE PERSON.

How a speaker starts a presentation will have a significant impact on how the audience perceives that speaker and how they respond to his presentation. Many speakers tend to look at the audience and take them in all at once, which can make the speaker appear lost and perhaps dazed by the situation in which he finds himself. Other speakers avoid looking at the audience altogether and simply focus on their notes, talking to the podium or to their cards. Neither of these starts projects any confidence or control to the audience.

President Ronald Reagan was once asked why he was known as the 'great communicator'. He responded with a question to the reporter. What do you think is the largest group that I have ever spoken to? The reporter surmised that it must be in the hundreds of thousands to which Reagan responded, "Nope." The reporter stated that there were more than that at the Republican National Convention and Reagan told him that was not the point.

"The largest audience that I have ever spoken to is one. I learned a long time ago that when I try to talk to everyone, I communicate with no one. When I talk to one person, I communicate with everyone."

This is a good lesson for all of us to learn. Looking up and locking in with one person helps a speaker to set the pace of his presentation and gives him the focus that he needs to connect with the audience. Instead of seeing an audience as a single mass or a sea of bodies, speakers need to learn to see that audience as a group of diverse individuals, each of whom is looking to make that personal connection.

This process also helps to set the tone of the presentation. Many speakers become better as they progress into their presentation. If they fail to connect with the audience at the beginning and present a jerky start to the presentation by darting glances between cards and across the sea of bodies, their message may well lose its impact. After the initial contact and pace is established the speaker can then begin to adjust his eye contact from one person to the next.

The smoothness of his start projects the speaker's confidence and control and commands the attention of the audience. If you fail to communicate with an audience as individuals, you will never make the connection necessary to influence them toward your vision or purpose. To achieve success, you must have confidence in yourself and believe in what you are there to communicate. This is the first step.

21

BEGIN AND END WITH A SMILE.

There is nothing more uncomfortable than sitting in an audience watching a presenter who is uncomfortable as a public speaker. As he fidgets and projects all types of behavior that tell us he is uncomfortable, we begin to get nervous and anxious for him. This takes our focus off a speaker and his message; we just want to see him get through his presentation without being embarrassed.

As I mentioned before, the speaker sets the tone for his presentation and the audience looks to him for clues to give them a sense of what to expect. Of the 7000 facial expressions that humans are capable of producing, we use only a small portion of them (a few hundred) to express ourselves. Audiences are looking for these expressions to determine the mood of a speaker's presentation.

Expressions produce a feeling inside us; as our facial expressions change, so too does the feeling that is generated within us. Smiles work for us in two ways. As we are preparing to deliver our presentation, if we are smiling and stimulating a feeling of well being within ourselves, then we will generate a similar feeling on the part of our audience. By contrast, if we are obsessing and frowning, we will generate the emotion associated with these expressions. Facial expressions are contagious. As we make contact with an audience and smile, they will naturally smile back. This relaxes the audience and prepares them to receive the speaker's message. A smile tells the audience that you want to be there and that you are in control so they can sit back and relax while you take them on a journey that you are well-prepared to conduct. On the other hand, a stern or serious look sets the mood that may as well be saying to an audience, 'stand by, this is going to be a stormy ride.'

As we wrap up our presentation, we want to close with the same feeling of comfort that we opened with, letting our audience know that we have said exactly what we wanted to say and we are comfortable with our presentation. This is why we always want to leave them with a smile on their faces.

It is in our interest to set the tone of our entire presentation by opening and closing with a smile. The audience does not want to be uncomfortable and you don't want them to be uncomfortable. Use those pearly whites to their full potential and begin and end with a smile.

22

YOU NEVER GET A SECOND CHANCE TO MAKE A FIRST IMPRESSION.

This is something that many of our fathers and mothers told us over and over again as we were growing up. The problem we run into is that during our formative years, we are in school and being influenced day in and day out by our peers. During this time, we are trying very hard to fit in. This need to fit in with our peers drives us to be part of a culture of rebellion.

Few teens like to do anything the way their parents do; most teens are driven by a desire to fit in with and impress their friends. This can present big problems after high school when, as young adults, they are now required to function in the real world. Often these young adults find that what worked for them in high school isn't cutting it in the general society. They may have already developed habits that worked great in the microcosm of the school grounds but, in the real world, are actually detractors to their success.

In the real world it takes about 3 to 5 seconds to develop a first impression. This first impression is 95 percent accurate based upon the life experience that the person developing the impression brings to the table. Those who have seen enough of life to know what right looks like and what wrong looks like tend to immediately place people and things into a category based upon their own past experiences and the recognized cultural norms of the society. We must be careful that as we try to do things that will make us stand out, these do not become detractors that put us in a box that is categorized as unfavorable or undesirable. While tattoos, body piercings, bad posture, inappropriate jewelry, non-traditional attire, lack of eye contact, use of pop culture expressions and so forth are all examples of self-expression, an audience is going to use every element that a presenter gives them to develop that impression within three to five seconds. After they have formulated that first impression, the audience will see only what they want to see. Everything they gather from that point on serves to support that first impression and backs up their initial determination to be influenced or not influenced by the speaker's message.

Understanding how we look from the audience's perspective is vitally important. If we do not look the part that the audience expects to see, then we instantly come under intense scrutiny as they search frantically to discover what makes you and, consequently, your message credible and relevant to their lives. As mentioned earlier, people are looking to the visual elements far more than the words we say to determine the credibility of our message. So the next time you set out to make an impression on someone, take a look at yourself in a mirror and ask yourself; What does my appearance say to my audience? You'll never get a second chance to make that first impression.

23

DO NOT LOOK AT NOTES FOR FIRST OR LAST 10 PERCENT OF A PRESENTATION.

The introduction and conclusion are the most memorable parts of any presentation and this is where the appeal has to be placed in order to have the most powerful impact upon our audience. Because it is so important to make a personal connection with the audience, speakers must open and close with a message from the heart. What this means is that, as speakers, we must open strong and close strong and present with passion and conviction. This is hard to do if we are reading from our notes, trying to make sure that we cover all of the statistical data that we have included in our presentation.

Many speakers who are uncomfortable have a tendency to use their notes as a crutch. Introductions often include basic biographical data about the speaker or a brief introduction into what the presentation is going to cover. This is data that is well known by the speaker and should require no notes to reference. There is nothing that destroys the power of a presentation more than a speaker who looks at his notes during the introduction as if to make sure he pronounces his own name correctly.

This also holds true if a speaker refers to his notes as he concludes his presentation as though he does not remember what he has just spoken about. There are few things that project a lack of confidence in and knowledge about the material we have just presented more than having to look to our notes as we are calling our audience to action. How is it possible to influence others when we cannot even remember what it is that we have just said? If the message is important to us, then we know exactly what we want from our audience and it is not necessary to look at our notes to remind us.

The conclusion of a presentation is our last opportunity to leave the audience with a WIIFM (What's In It For Me) and this needs to come from the heart. It is hard to appear as though you are speaking from the heart if you are reading from your notes, making sure to use the exact verbiage you have written. Like a poor actor reading a cue card, the speaker loses the impact of his message when it is just words being read from a card.

Speakers generally know what they want to say during the introduction and conclusion of their presentation but habitual dependence upon notes will detract from the most important parts of that presentation. If you feel that you must refer to notes during a presentation, wait until you get through the introduction and then be sure to put them away as you move into your conclusion. This will help to eliminate the possibility of looking to your notes out of nervousness or habit. To maintain the power of your presentation, refrain from looking at your notes for the first or last 10 percent of your presentation.

#24

RULES OF CARDS

Regular 3 by 5 cards are great tools for any speaker. They are small and easy to carry. They fit into the palm of your hand, allowing for the use of hand gestures. They are less distracting than a paper outline. Lastly, they travel with us as we move and interact with the audience. As with any notes, however, there are some rules that will make them more effective and will help us avoid some common pitfalls.

WRITE ON THE CARDS VERTICALLY RATHER THAN HORIZONTALLY

This helps us in two ways. First, it ensures that we do not write our ideas in sentence format because there just is not sufficient space. We must always be careful about what we write on our cards because if we take the time to write something then we will feel a need to read it word for word. This takes away the 'quick reference' purpose of the cards. Reading sentences slows us down and looks awkward. It turns the notes into a crutch rather than an enhancement to our presentation. By keeping our notes down to ideas rather than sentences, we are not tempted to read them.

The second thing that writing on the cards vertically does for us is to project an image of confidence. How we hold the cards to read them is noticed by the audience; glancing at the cards in our palm presents a much more polished look than holding the card horizontally to read what we have written.

NO MORE THAN 3 IDEAS/LINES PER CARD

Write large enough to see what you have written easily. There is nothing worse than watching someone who has transposed an entire sheet of notes onto a 3 by 5 card attempting to find his place in what he wants to say.

NUMBER YOUR CARDS (CENTER TOP)

If we drop our cards or they get out of order, we need to ensure that we can easily get them back into order without much distraction.

CARDS IN ONE HAND

Cards can become a crutch and distraction if speakers are not properly trained how to use them. Holding the cards in two hands in front of us creates a barrier between us and the audience. Amateur speakers sometimes use the cards to create barriers in place of larger objects such as podiums or tables. Also, if we hold our cards in two hands, we tend to start playing with them, also creating a distraction.

WRITE ON ONE SIDE

The preparation for a presentation is not the time to go green. Do not complicate things for yourself by writing on both sides of your cards. This will only make it more difficult to find your spot if you lose your place and can make it very difficult to follow your notes.

25

EYE CONTACT

The eyes have it. Many cultures believe that the eyes are the windows to the soul and they are of major significance in how people look at one another. In the American culture it is customary to look people in the eye when speaking to them. Failure by a speaker to look an audience in the eye can be interpreted in three ways. One, the speaker is not interested in whether or not the audience hears what he is saying; two, the speaker is lying and is uncomfortable because he is afraid he will be found out; or three, the speaker lacks confidence and is simply unable to look people in the eye. Regardless of the interpretation, lack of eye contact works to the detriment of the speaker.

Eye contact is an important behavioral indicator that police evaluate as they interview suspects to determine deception during an investigation. When people are being deceptive, their external behavior reflects their internal anxiety as they attempt to hide their deception and not be discovered. Remembering that audiences are very perceptive on a conscious and subconscious level, we realize that even though they may not be questioning why a speaker is not looking at them, they do understand that something is not right. In order to make sure that we are not misinterpreted, we must simply follow a few rules.

HOLD EYE CONTACT 3 TO 5 SECONDS

Holding eye contact with one person at a time, for 3 to 5 seconds, tells the audience that a speaker recognizes them as individuals; less than three seconds indicates that he sees them as an audience but not as individual people. With his eyes darting around the room, the speaker appears to be frantically attempting to avoid a true connection with anyone in the audience.

Just as we may not hold eye contact long enough, we may also hold it too long as well. After five seconds, people begin to feel uncomfortable, as though the speaker is singling them out from the rest of the audience. We never want to make our audience feel uncomfortable. Some reasons that we hold eye contact with someone for more than five seconds may be because we are attracted to them or perhaps we see that person as a threat and are about to engage in a confrontation with them.

95 PERCENT OF THE TIME

We should be looking at the audience 95 percent of the time we spend in front of that audience. The only time a speaker might not be looking at the audience is when he is referring to his notes. A speaker who ignores his audience gives the appearance that the audience has permission to ignore him as well. Avoiding eye contact with an audience is a sure way to lose influence with them.

SWEEP THE CORNERS

Make sure you look at everyone. Speakers often develop a pattern of eye movement within the audience that seems to ignore people on the fringes. Great speakers make sure they draw in the entire audience with their eye contact. It is hard to ignore someone who is looking directly at you, so to ensure that you engage the entire audience, remember these rules of eye contact.

26

LIFE IS A WORLD CUP WITH NO TIMEOUTS. YOU ARE ALWAYS ON!

For all world-class performers, every minute of every day is game on. Those who believe that great performances can be turned on and off like a light switch are sadly mistaken, much to their detriment. Our performance as a presenter is a reflection of our habits and our habits are the by-product of our day-in-and-day-out execution. People who do a thing right are people who generally do it right all the time; and people who do it wrong are generally people who do a thing wrong all the time. Excellence is the by-product of thousands of tiny details coming together to produce consistent superior results. This is not an accident nor is it easy to achieve.

Our actions are almost always being judged and evaluated by others. While we judge ourselves on our intentions we judge others on their actions. To ensure top performance, we need to live our lives every day in an excellent manner. Regardless of what we are doing or who is watching, we need to do what is right and perform every action in the very best way that we can, taking full responsibility for our actions and the outcomes of our actions. If we can train ourselves to live our lives in this manner, we will be constantly preparing ourselves to make the best possible responses under pressure.

We are always being evaluated by the qualities or outcomes that we produce in life. What kind of qualities do you produce in your kids, your family life, your work, your relationships, your hobbies, and your spare time? All of these are results of your daily efforts and we are judged and evaluated by how well we perform in these areas. We may tell ourselves that this is all personal and is nobody's business but it is impossible to separate these elements in our lives. It is human nature to use all the information available to us to evaluate a situation and attempt to predict future performance. This is how we identify potential in people. This does not mean that we are perfect. It simply means that people who are attempting to perform well in every aspect of their lives all the time are seen as motivated and focused while those who are not trying to do this are often interpreted as being lazy and lacking discipline.

Working toward excellence in every aspect of our lives is a lifelong pursuit that begins with the first step. What steps are you going to take in your life today to begin moving you toward an excellent life? We must live our lives as if each of us is in a world cup event with no timeouts. We are always on!

27

REMOVE ALL DISTRACTERS FROM BELTS, POCKETS AND BODY BEFORE SPEAKING.

There are so many things that can distract an audience. As speakers, it is our responsibility to remove as many of these distractions as possible. Some speakers go to great lengths to reduce the number of distracters in the environment by managing the setting so the audience is facing away from windows, by removing posters, or by closing doors to hallways, only to neglect to look at themselves in a mirror. The items we wear on our person can become distracters. If the audience is distracted, they are not paying attention to the speaker or his message. We do not want to be a part of the problem by being unaware of how we ourselves are providing distracters.

When we are speaking, we are attempting to command the audience's attention and focus it on the speaker's face. The face is the most expressive element for displaying our feelings and the moods we want to project. We need the audience to pay close attention to every facial gesture so that they can see and properly interpret our meaning.

Speakers can become their own worst enemy by wearing items that demand attention from and cause speculation by the audience. Badges are a classic example. If a speaker is wearing any sort of corporate or organizational identification badge during a presentation, the audience tends to feel obliged to try to read it and speculate about the speaker's position.

Cell phones or other items hanging on the belt also can give rise to speculation. Is that a company phone? Did the department pay for it? Why doesn't my department pay for phones? I wonder how many minutes they get? Why do they get the new phones? If members of the audience are asking themselves these questions, they are not listening to the speaker or paying attention to his message.

Many professional military personnel actually do self-inspections prior to standing before a class, removing expensive watches, medals, badges, phones, knives, change from pockets, keys and other items to ensure that they are bringing no distracters to the podium with them. It is difficult enough to maintain the attention of an audience without providing your own distracters.

Every member of an audience is a Sherlock Holmes of sorts. Each one is scrutinizing every aspect of the speaker all the time in an attempt to gain more information on which to judge his credibility. The level of credibility that the audience gives the speaker will determine the level of influence the speaker's message is going to have in their lives. Don't be your own worst enemy. Conduct a self-inspection and remove all distracters before going before an audience.

28

HAND GESTURES SHOULD SUPPORT, REINFORCE AND BACK UP OUR WORDS.

Listless speakers produce listless audiences and a good way to avoid this is through the use of hand gestures. Insecure speakers, in their desire to protect themselves from their audience, are constantly trying to put something between themselves and the audience. It can be an object such as a podium, a chair or a table or it can be space the speaker uses as a barrier by standing as far away from the audience as possible. It is as if the speaker believes that by maintaining distance from the audience, his flaws will be invisible to them. The last line of defense may be the clasping of his hands in front by the speaker and sometimes holding cards or notes.

Great communicators go to great lengths to remove the barriers between themselves and their audiences. They do not want anything that will keep them from being able to make a connection with the audience they want to touch. Knowing that audiences gain so much of their information from visual cues, it is incumbent upon us as communicators to develop a style of delivery that projects what we are saying through our hand gestures. This is a developed skill that few speakers take to naturally.

When we are beginning to use hand gestures, we must think about what kind of gestures we are going to use and at what point they will be most effective during our presentation. Failure to plan this into our presentation may result in a very static delivery. When we use hand gestures we want them to be big. This is how we create dynamics in our presentation. Also remember that higher is better than lower. In an attempt to reveal as little as possible about himself to the audience, a speaker may perform hand gestures at waist level, waving his hands around to create a pattern or a rhythm that helps him feel more comfortable. These measures are very distracting to an audience.

Hand gestures should be appropriate and at face level. This is where we want the audience to focus. There is nothing happening below my belt that I want the audience to focus on so I am not going to do anything that is going to draw their attention to this area. Audiences want to see energy and dynamics from a speaker and the best way to produce this is through the use of hand gestures that support, reinforce and back up what we are saying.

29

START YOUR DAY WITH AN AFFIRMATION.

Affirmations are a simple tool that can help us to get ourselves on the right course mentally at the start of each day. Words have power and we can use the power of words to determine how we respond to things that occur throughout the day. Everything in life is a matter of perspective and our own individual perspective will influence how we respond to situations in our life every day. There is an old proverb that says: *Nothing is good or bad lest we think it.* Situations just are what they are. They would still be the same even if we had no knowledge of them. We give situations titles and power based on our view of them and how they impact us.

Our attitude toward situations and events is extremely powerful. We have little or no control over the actions of others but we do have control over how we perceive and will respond to the events in our lives and to the actions of others in response to those events.

There are three parts to an affirmation. First, the affirmation must be **a statement in the positive**. We don't want to start out condemning our day to doom and gloom. If we state that it is going to be a HORRIBLE day, then guess what? That is what we expect to find so we see everything in the context of not being good. Our perspective provides context to how we will perceive events. Words have power to program our subconscious and we use this power to find exactly what we look for. Start your day with a statement in the positive so that you will see the opportunity in every situation.

Second, an affirmation **must be stated or written**. It is not enough to just think the affirmation. We must say it out loud or write it down. There must be a physical act associated with our affirmation. This process helps to bring our outside in alignment with our inside.

Third, the affirmation **must be repeated**. It is not enough to say it or write it only once. We must repeat our affirmation until we believe it and ensure that it is the leading force in our day. Start every day with an affirmation.

It is going to be a great day!

30

THE 3 "P"s OF VOICE

In face-to-face communications the voice or vocal aspect carries 38 percent of the message that we want to deliver to our audience. This number increases dramatically if we are speaking over the telephone or on the radio. Because of this we must pay special attention to how we use this precious tool. How we verbalize our message will determine how it will be interpreted by an audience. We do this every day ourselves as we listen to the way in which someone asks us to do something or how information is being provided to us. How something gets said determines how we feel about the message. We can feel as though we are being lectured to or are being helped based on the subtle vocal variations that a speaker uses to provide that information.

Where a speaker puts the emphasis in a sentence can determine the meaning of the entire sentence. Untrained speakers often try to protect themselves from being vulnerable to their audiences by speaking in a monotone and eliminating any vocal variation. In this way they are trying to take all of the emphasis off themselves and put it on the message. What they are really doing, however, is being boring and destroying the effectiveness of their presentation. The audience now has no way to know what is important and they may even stop listening after just a few sentences. In order to command the audience's attention we must use the three Ps of our voice:

PITCH
POWER
PACE

Pitch is going from very high to very low in the tone we use in the delivery of our message. Power is volume that we add to our vocal quality, moving from speaking very quietly to speaking very loudly. Learning how to move appropriately from a whisper to a near shout can be a very effective way to grab the audience's attention. Pace is the tempo at which we deliver our presentation. We want to move from speaking very slowly to very rapidly to put emphasis on various parts of our presentation. Slowing our pace places focus on our message and draws the audience in.

Like all habits, learning to use the three Ps of our voice appropriately involves a conscious process of change. To be effective as a presenter we must learn to use our voice to its full potential.

31

MARTIN LUTHER KING'S KEYS TO AN EFFECTIVE PRESENTATION

Dr. Martin Luther King, Jr., is noted for many memorable presentations because he had mastered the art of connecting with the audience. Dr. King used four key principles to capture the attention of his audience and help them to retain his message long after he was finished with his delivery.

START STRONG
END STRONG
THEME REPETITION
SPEAK WITH PASSION

The first thing that any speaker needs to do is grab the attention of the audience. This takes advantage of what is known as the 'primacy effect'. People have a tendency to remember the first thing they hear so we want to choose our opening words carefully to ensure that they convey exactly what we want our audience to remember.

Second, we want to end strong. This takes advantage of the 'recency effect'. An audience also is likely to remember the last thing they hear from the speaker. Because of this we want to end our presentation with a good take-away.

The third thing we want to do is employ theme repetition. As speakers, it is incumbent upon us to develop the message that we want the audience to remember. By developing a theme, we tell the audience what we think is important for them to remember and we need to drive home that theme repeatedly during the presentation. Dr. King was so good at this that many of his speeches are remembered for their theme even more than for the purpose of his presentation.

Themes give the audience an easy take-away and that is what we want as a speaker. Remember, it is not so much what you say as a speaker that matters, it only matters what the audience takes away. Giving the audience a take-away is the speaker's responsibility. This is sometimes referred to as making the presentation 'sticky' or memorable. We want our message to 'stick' so, as speakers, we need to come up with a theme that the audience can easily remember and then use it repeatedly throughout our presentation.

Lastly, we must speak with passion. Passion drives the message. Presentations are nothing more than statistics and information if we do not infuse them with our own passion. We cannot move an audience to action without moving them first to emotion and the way to do this is to show them our passion for the message. Our passion inspires and empowers people to take action and this is what we are trying to do as influencers. Most people are not naturally skilled at this process so while you are in the planning stage of your program, strive to develop Dr. Martin Luther King's keys to an effective presentation and incorporate them into your delivery.

32

DO THE THING YOU FEAR, AND THE THING YOU FEAR WILL DISAPPEAR.

Most of us avoid the things we fear. Our instinct is to move away from things that make us feel uncomfortable or seem dangerous. Things that make us uncomfortable but aren't necessarily dangerous are often just phobias. A phobia is an irrational fear of something. The key word here is irrational. We are talking about something that prevents us from functioning when in a particular environment.

Public speaking is listed as a fear by more people than any other human activity. Some even fear public speaking more than they do death. In other words, they would rather be dead than to have to give the eulogy. It is a tragedy that one of the most important skills we can have in terms of determining our future success is feared by so many. There are two reasons for this. One reason is lack of training. Most people know a good presentation when they see it but few people actually understand the specific elements of a good presentation.

What makes a presentation good or bad? Many of us took speech classes in high school and college that may have taught us little more than how to write a speech and stand up behind the podium and read it. We come to believe that some people have the gift of public speaking and some people do not. The truth is that most great speakers were at one time poor speakers. They simply have had the advantage of training whether through experience or in a formal classroom environment.

Another reason that many people fear public speaking is that they have so little opportunity to do it and may even avoid it when the opportunity arises. This lack of familiarity with the process can become a slippery slope toward future avoidance as we fall into a cycle of justifying why we do not like public speaking.

Two key elements that will help us to overcome the fear of public speaking are training and practice. Training helps us to understand the process in a safe and supportive environment and allows us to gain feedback without risk to our ego. This is the first step in the stress-inoculation process. We fear the unknown; as the unknown becomes familiar, we are less and less afraid of it. Practice helps us to gain the experience we need to continue to develop in the specific environments in which we are working. Not all public speaking environments are the same. There are subtle differences that a speaker must take into consideration and adapt to in order to be an effective communicator. If we want to grow and develop, we must force ourselves to do the thing we fear, and the thing we fear will disappear.

33

UNTIL I TRY TO DO SOMETHING I HAVE NOT ALREADY MASTERED, I WILL NOT GROW.

The process of learning is as important as what we learn. Self-awareness is an important aspect of personal development. For most of us, the process of learning requires effort and as humans we generally avoid things that require effort. This is especially true when it comes to the effort of thinking. This is why we develop habits in our lives so that we can avoid the effort of having to think every minute about what we are doing and instead just do it as part of a natural thought-less process. To fully understand ourselves, we must also understand how we learn and, in particular, how we learn best.

There are many methods by which we take in information. Learning is a process of interpreting and retaining our sensory input. We gain information through auditory, visual or kinesthetic functions. Research has shown that the more senses we use in the learning process, the higher the probability will be that we will retain the information for a longer period of time. This is why, as speakers, we should do everything in our power to engage as many of the senses as possible when we are trying to influence an audience to learn something from our message.

The learning process is like any process that we apply ourselves to and practice daily. We are going to grow and get better as we recognize our strengths and weaknesses and work toward identifying our ideal learning process. For some people, this may mean reading and taking notes or underlining information in a book. For others, this may mean listening to a lecture on tape repeatedly. And still others may need to go out and actually experience the hands-on of the process to fully understand and retain what is being taught.

Many students do not learn in a classroom. What I mean by this is that for many students, the classroom is a place where they simply identify what it is that they need to retain. When they leave the classroom, they use the method best suited to their learning style to begin the process of developing retention. Because of this, instructors need to be careful about the practice of teaching and then giving surprise quizzes immediately after the lesson. Many students have not even begun the process of learning the material at this point; and forcing them to show what they have retained can produce negative results, including animosity toward the instructor and low student self-esteem because of a poor performance on these quizzes.

The better we understand how we learn best and the more we refine our learning tactics, the better chance we have of changing the process of learning from a chore to a joy, a process by which we can grow and develop. The more we learn, the more we understand how things are inter-related in life. This knowledge allows us to synergize the opportunities that are presented to us and to take advantage of this power as we seek to influence our audiences to learn something, to follow a vision or to buy our products. Learning helps us grow and until we learn to do something that we have not already mastered, we will not grow.

#34

WHATEVER THE MIND CAN CONCEIVE AND THE HEART CAN BELIEVE, THE BODY CAN ACHIEVE.

We have the ability to do whatever we desire in life but there is a catch. In order to achieve our goals we must first understand the relationship between the mind, the heart and the body, the three interrelated components of success in anything that we choose to do in life. Our thoughts, our feelings and our physical ability are constantly communicating with one another; how they communicate says a lot about who we are. Our body is constantly receiving input from our external environment. Our heart is determining how we feel about that input and our mind is interpreting the data from our body and heart and making decisions about how we are going to deal with the input.

The mind is by far the most powerful of the influencers in this triad because ultimately everything else will submit to the will of the mind. The body, on the other hand, is the most submissive of the three, submitting itself to the will of the mind and heart. The mind determines what is acceptable and what is not. It sets the left and right boundaries for what is right and what is wrong in any given situation. If our body says that it is straining or that it is hurt or cold, the mind then determines if this is an acceptable amount of stress for the body to deal with or if it is necessary to change the situation. Our heart is going to determine how we feel about the input and begin placing value on the level of acceptability that the mind has decided the body should be willing to tolerate in the given situation.

These three elements are in a constant struggle and the outcome of that struggle will determine our actions. Our actions are the primary determiners of our success. As an example, we may know what the right thing to do is but often we do not feel like doing it so we avoid it or choose not to give it our best effort. In another case, we may feel that we want to do something but we lack the knowledge to be able to accomplish it. Finally, we may have the desire and knowledge but lack the necessary skills to be able to accomplish the task.

Success is a perfect combination of thought, feeling and ability. When we have a vision and a desire to drive toward that vision, we have begun the process of moving toward success. This does not necessarily mean that we have all the information or skills we need or that we will not question ourselves along the way, but when we can harmoniously focus our thoughts feelings and abilities toward a goal, we produce a synergistic power that will leave no room for failure.

Many people sabotage themselves in this process. Too often, when they come upon obstacles, they start to question themselves and this allows feelings of self-doubt to creep in. "Oh, I can't do this, what was I thinking?" "Who am I to be able to do this?" At this point, we talk ourselves directly into quitting. The problem with quitting is that we never know how close we were to success when we decide to give up. This is one of the reasons that it is so important to have outside moral support in our efforts. When we start to get down on ourselves, our friends, our loved ones and our family can help to get us back on track by helping us to realize the greatness within ourselves.

There is no greater gift that anyone can offer us than to inspire us toward our dreams and our vision. So next time you start to feel down or you begin to question yourself, remember this thought: feelings and abilities must work in harmony with one another in order for us to achieve our goal. What the mind can conceive and the heart can believe, the body can achieve.

35

LUCK IS WHEN PLANNING AND PREPARATION INTERSECT OPPORTUNITY.

Vince Lombardi was once told by a reporter how lucky he was. In frustration the coach responded. "You're right! I am lucky. I am the luckiest guy in the world." Then he clarified his statement. "Do you know what luck is?" he asked the reporter". Luck is when planning and preparation intersect opportunity. That is what luck is and you are right. I am the luckiest guy in the world."

Lombardi understood the true meaning of what it is to be lucky. Luck is not an accident of fate or a pick of the lottery. Luck is part of a process and the better we understand the process, the more likely it is that we will succeed or be 'lucky'. First we have to understand what we are trying to accomplish and then we need to have a plan to support that goal. Would it surprise you to know that just by having a clearly defined goal we are more likely to achieve it than if we do not have a goal? There are many reasons why people do not set goals in their lives. For some it is because they fear failure and for others it is because it would force them to change an existing pattern of behavior. It is much safer to go though life without goals but it really is much less rewarding. We must learn to take risks in life if we are going to experience life to the fullest.

Once we have a goal and a plan then we must prepare for an opportunity to achieve the goal. This is a daily process of working toward a goal. As we do this, we are creating endless opportunities that will allow us to move closer to what we want to achieve. The planning and preparation are the time-consuming parts of any goal but they are the greatest determiners of our success. Opportunity may be limited to the cycle of events in our lives but planning and preparation are parts of a never-ending process.

True professionals never stop training, planning and preparing. This is one of the marks of a world-class performer in any field of life. Thomas Edison once said that accomplishment is one percent inspiration and 99 percent perspiration. Thoughts are abundant and a part of life but action is what is needed to move beyond this stage. Planning and preparation will bring you closer to any goal you set. Luck is when planning and preparation intersect opportunity. I am the luckiest man alive.

36

SUCCESS LEAVES CLUES.

Become a tracker of excellences. The trail to success or failure is marked by the choices made and the actions and reactions taken by individuals as they move toward a point where they eventually find themselves. These elements leave signs or clues. Regardless of how new or innovative your concept, someone who came before you likely has accomplished something similar to it using a framework that may fit your game plan perfectly. As we are developing our planning, it is to our advantage to find people who have accomplished similar goals to those we have set for ourselves and take a close look at how they did it. How did they live their lives? What skills did they need to learn? What were the tools they needed? How did they organize their resources? How long did it take? How did they manage their time? What hurdles did they have to overcome?

This works to our advantage in three ways. One, having a mentor provides us with a template by which to measure our progress toward our goal. Seeing our progression is important because it helps to keep us motivated. Two, having a mentor gives us a good reality check of the timeline we can expect to maintain. Being over-optimistic can be just as dangerous as being under-optimistic. Three, we can learn a lot from the hurdles and pitfalls that others have faced. We can benefit from their experiences to avoid some of the hardships they had to endure.

As we examine the careers of people who have achieved great things in life, it is easy to become fixated on the accomplishment itself and fail to recognize that the achievement is the result of years of work. We may not be aware of the sacrifice, discipline, difficult choices, hard work, pain or struggle that successful people have undergone to accomplish their goals. If we truly want to accomplish our own goals, we must become good trackers and learn to see the path that those who have successfully walked it before us have laid out.

It has been said that if we have a glimpse of greatness, it is because we have stood upon the shoulders of those who have come before us. Take advantage of that high ground and learn from those forerunners what they did right as well as what they did wrong. In summary, we can recognize some of the obstacles before us and avoid them as we move forward on our journey. Success leaves clues and to become successful ourselves, we must become expert trackers.

37

AVOID QUALIFIERS.

As speakers, we put great value on accuracy. We don't want to make a mistake or have our words misinterpreted because this will lead to doubts about our concepts or ideas. The fear of being called to the mat or questioned causes some presenters to want to build a safety net into their presentations. This safety net often comes in the form of qualifiers.

Qualifiers are subtle ways in which we modify the power or strength of our presentation to ensure that what we say is not overly optimistic giving us too-high expectations. Qualifiers often come in the form of a catchall phrase that relieves the speaker of any responsibility if for some reason the concept or plan he has presented does not work. As a presenter, the more your subject matter relies on accuracy, the more you are likely to fall into the qualifier trap. If you are a teacher, scientist, doctor, or engineer, then you may be particularly susceptible to using qualifiers.

This is not to say that there are not times when the use of qualifiers is justified but it is important to understand when it is the right place and time for this.

For teachers, qualifiers may be appropriate to use as they attempt to teach flexible thinking and an understanding of variables. Leaders and sales representatives, however, lose credibility when they wrap up with qualifiers. Even if the audience does not focus on the qualifier being used, they notice it and record it subconsciously. Words such as 'could', 'possibly', 'should', 'might', 'I believe', 'I think', and 'likely' are all qualifiers that we have a tendency to use when we are unsure of something. This tactic provides us with a built-in excuse just in case what we are saying does not fix the problem, resolve the issue or provide the promised outcome.

The main problem with using qualifiers is that they take away from a presenter's credibility rather than reinforcing it. Being a leader means having to take responsibility and with this responsibility comes risk. Speakers who use qualifiers are attempting to mitigate their responsibility by building an escape route into their presentation with phrases such as 'could work', 'might work', 'should work'.

Audiences understand that with every plan comes risk. They are looking to a leader who is willing to take responsibility and is confident enough to accept the risk without building in an escape route. We must become confident and comfortable using words like 'will', 'can' and 'know' rather than employing qualifiers. When you are putting together a presentation, accept your responsibility as a leader and avoid the use of qualifiers.

38

IT IS TEN TIMES WORSE TO LOOK UP THAN DOWN.

Looking is one of those habitual actions that most presenters never think about. Unless a speaker works with a professional trainer, he probably never will recognize the effect this has on an audience and how they will receive a presentation. Looking up is one of those very small actions by a speaker that projects volumes to the audience. In glancing upwards, he seems to be seeking heavenly comfort as if searching for that guidance that can come only from the Almighty in our time of need.

Looking up by a speaker can be seen even from the back of an auditorium. Eye contact is very important to an audience. They are looking for those subtle signs that will give them insight into how they should feel about a speaker and his subsequent presentation. When we are standing up in front of an audience and we hit that mental block and are not sure what we are going to say next, we will often instinctively look for divine intervention to impart wisdom upon us. As we do so, we glance upward and telegraph to the entire audience that we have just forgotten what it was we wanted to say at this point and are frantically searching for the words to fill the horrible ensuing silence that is now coming over the audience as they anxiously wait to see if we are going to pull out of this deadly tailspin or are we going to dive right into the ground.

As horrible as this moment is for any speaker, it has an even more devastating impact on an audience. The audience now knows that the speaker is working from memory and that his message is not coming from the heart. They understand that they are on the receiving end of a prepared presentation that the speaker is showing signs of having forgotten. They begin to empathize with the speaker's anxiety and are now nervous about what is going to happen next.

If you have ever had to sit and listen to a poor speaker, you know the anxiety I am talking about here, as you wait for the speaker to impale himself upon a stake provided by his own words. The audience is no longer paying any attention to the message and instead is hoping with every fiber of their being that the hapless speaker does not make a fool of himself. They do not want to be witness to his embarrassment any more than he wants to be embarrassed.

Remember that an audience has no idea of what we want to say or what we may be going to say. It is not as if they are watching a rerun of a presentation. This is their first exposure to the material being presented by the speaker. The problem is that if we are well rehearsed and we know what we want to say we can become flustered if we forget and frantically search our memories for the exact words in the exact order that we have practiced. The key is to not become so fixated on the exact verbiage or the precise order of our presentation that we leave ourselves no flexibility to let our words flow freely as we speak from the heart.

If you get lost, just flow with it and keep on going. Don't worry that you don't have the exact words that you used during practice or that you have lost track of what came next in the order of your presentation. Simply pause for a moment and go to your notes and smoothly transition into your next point. Inside, we will be frustrated and may feel as though we have blown it but we never want to project this dissatisfaction with our own performance to the audience. This is why it is ten times worse to look up than down.

39

GET OUT OF THE BOX.

Nothing commands the attention of the audience like movement around the stage on the part of the speaker. It is unpredictable and requires an audience pay attention to see where the speaker is going. I don't mean the kind of box-step designed to fake out an audience and make it look as though the speaker is moving; I am talking about that get-out-and-wade-into-the-audience kind of movement. Many untrained speakers have a tendency to develop a rhythmic movement consisting of one or two steps in either direction that gives the appearance of movement but is not real movement. This is still staying in that box and it says to the audience: I am unsure of myself and am going to stay right here in my comfort zone. Many speakers attempt to place barriers between themselves and their audience and one of these barriers is distance.

There are many barriers that speakers must become aware of. Most of these barriers are located in the subconscious rather than being actual barriers. As an example, I have seen speakers who were not able to move beyond a certain point in a room because a pronounced seam in the carpet created a subconscious boundary that they would not cross. I have also seen speakers who would not cross a line of tape that had been placed on the stage for a previous event. Some speakers will not move forward past the first row of chairs into the room as though they were approaching a black hole from which they would not be able to return. When confronted and asked why they would not move past these identified lines, most of these speakers were not even aware of what they had done.

This is the kind of thing that happens when we are under stress. Our subconscious tries to help us out by interpreting things for us and causing us to react in such a way that we do not have to take our mind off the task at hand. The mind is very powerful and as it identifies these seams, tapes and invisible lines, it can interpret them as barriers that restrict the speaker's movement to a particular area. The only way to overcome this is to recognize these 'barriers' ahead of time and consciously decide how and where to move past them. Not doing so may result in a speaker becoming a prisoner to his subconscious reaction to artificial barriers.

Great speakers know that the best way to command the attention of the audience is to move in and get close with them. They will often go to great lengths to create an environment that allows them to move into a part of their audience without losing contact with the rest of the audience. Be creative and command the attention of your audience. Get out of the box.

40

WE MAKE A LIVING BY WHAT WE GET; WE MAKE A LIFE BY WHAT WE GIVE.

We all have to work in life and the compensation we receive for the work determines our standard of living. This process is often referred to as making a living. It is the process that sustains us by enabling us to own a house, purchase the clothes we need, pay for transportation and buy the comfort items that help us to feel better about ourselves.

But there is much more to life than just making a living. Few people will be remembered for how they made a living. It is a necessity of life. We all have to do it or we will die because of an inability to obtain the resources we need to survive. What we remember people for is how they make a life. Making a life is much more complicated than making a living. It is not about how much money we make, or the way we make it, or what we buy with it. It is not measured by the size of our house or the cost of our car. Making a life is about our interaction with others and more specifically what we give to others. This does not necessarily mean giving money, although this might be a part of it. There is so much of ourselves that we have to share. We can share our wisdom, knowledge, time, love, caring, concern, efforts, support, encouragement, honesty and much more. What we share with others is what defines us as people.

What we do, how we make a living, is not who we are. In the American culture, it is customary to ask others what they do as a matter of casual conversation. We put great emphasis on this and often use it in part to define other persons. In many foreign cultures, this is considered very rude. It is not polite to ask people what they do. People are not what they do.

We need to focus on who people are and the way to discover this is to understand how they make a life. What do they share with others? Do they care about people? What we share with others says much more about us than what we do for a living does. Life is about people, it is not about things. It is said that you can tell a lot about a leader by how he treats the lowest individual in his organization. How we treat people regardless of their status says a lot about who we are. Many people only treat others well when they have something to gain from them. In order to understand this, you must ask yourself two questions. How do you treat people who have nothing to offer you? How do you treat people who will never impact your life? The answers to these questions will tell you a lot about who you are. The more we understand this, the better we understand that we make a living by what we get but we make a life by what we give.

41

IT IS NOT A TRAGEDY TO DIE WITH DREAMS UNFULFILLED BUT IT IS A TRAGEDY TO DIE WITHOUT DREAMS.

There are only two states for all things in nature. One of them is growing and the other is dying. There is no such thing in nature as something being in a state of perfect stasis. This is the way we are as people; we are either growing or we are dying. Our growing is not just a physical process, it is also a mental process. Growing mentally is a byproduct of attitude. Some people stop growing at a very young age while others continue growing until they die of old age.

Part of this growing process is having dreams. Dreams are the mind's way of experiencing things that we have not yet achieved. They are God's way of showing us our destiny and giving us an idea of our potential. We have unlimited potential and sometimes our dreams are the only way we can see that. Dreams help to motivate us and they serve as a constant reminder of things we have yet to do in this life.

What we feel inside drives what we do outside and our dreams inspire us and drive us toward creating a future that we desire, a future that is better. Nobody dreams of being less than what they already are. Dreams offer a mental picture of where we want to be. Without dreams we are just going through the motions and getting through the day on the way to the grave. Our dreams challenge us to take risk, to try to do things we have never done, to attempt the impossible. They drive us to sacrifice for the future and to dare for what could be. They determine what actions we will take that are going to move us toward the mental image we have of ourselves.

Dreams are the very essence of life and when we stop dreaming, we have hopped onto the fast track to dying. This does not necessarily mean physical death. There are a lot of 'dead' people walking around in this world. They have had their dreams crushed and pushed deep down inside of them. They no longer even dare to dream for fear it will create more pain than happiness; they become comfortable living in a state of dying.

We hear many stories of people who have triumphed over those who would steal their dreams through oppression, torture, punishment and imprisonment. These people have endured beyond the limits of human suffering but they never gave up their dreams.

Dreams are on the inside. There is no outside force that can steal our dreams from us. The only way we can lose our dreams is to give them up. When we allow our own will to be subjugated to the will of others, we truly do die inside. We must never stop dreaming and we must never stop believing in our dreams. It is not a tragedy to die with dreams unfulfilled but it is a tragedy to die without dreams.

42

PASSION DRIVES THE MESSAGE BUT THERE MUST BE A UNIQUE BALANCE BETWEEN PASSION AND SUBSTANCE.

To connect with an audience, the speaker places a tremendous emphasis on stirring the passion of the audience. Because emotion moves the audience to action, the speaker who seeks to influence an audience must stir their emotions. We do this by exhibiting the passion that we want to see in our audience. As they observe our passion and conviction, they are encouraged to buy into our vision and act upon it.

Stirring the passion of an audience is an art that some people are better at than others. There is a catch, though. If the speaker's passion does not have a solid foundation rooted in factual data, it quickly subsides and the speaker loses credibility with those among his audience with the common sense necessary to question the rationale of the argument. Passion without substance will eventually fall flat. As we are stirring the passion of our audience, we must remember that they are thinking beings and while emotions may drive us, there does need to be a certain amount of evidence to support the logic of our claim.

Logic without passion, on the other hand, offers statistical information that will have very little impact on people's actions. Statistics is where speakers who are not comfortable with expressing themselves with excitement, energy and conviction generally go to hide from the audience. In an attempt to take the focus off themselves, they try to direct all of the audience's attention to the statistical information being presented.

It should be noted that there are many very good speakers who are able to stir the passions of an audience with little foundational evidence or fact to support their assertions. This generally short-lived excitement is designed to manipulate the audience in the short term to achieve a goal of the speaker. Passion may override logic for a while but eventually, thinking people will start to ask hard questions and they will expect to receive answers. If they don't get answers, they will ignore attempts by the speaker to influence their actions through his passion for the subject and start to seek out answers elsewhere.

Neither passion nor statistics have sufficient power independently to influence an audience in the long term. If we as leaders, salespeople, or teachers, are going to influence our audience, we must balance our passion with a solid foundation of fact and logic that has sufficient substance to support our emotional plea. If we do not do this, we may be judged as con men or snake oil salesmen. Once this has happened, it is almost impossible to get back the trust of our audience. Although passion may drive the message, the speaker must maintain a unique balance between passion and substance.

43

I MUST BECOME COMFORTABLE BEING UNCOMFORTABLE.

Being comfortable is overrated. There is nothing wrong with being uncomfortable. Discomfort is a gift that God has given us to help when we are under pressure. We are at our best when we are uncomfortable. Every nerve in our body is firing, our brain is in high gear and we are alert to anything that we may need to react to. When we start to get comfortable, we start to lose that edge and we stop trying so hard. We stop paying attention to the little details that make a big difference in our performance. If we become too familiar with certain environments, we relax and this is when mistakes happen.

When we relax too much, we lose our ability to maintain our cognitive focus. At this point, we have become too comfortable. This loss of situational awareness is common in anyone who has been doing something for a long period of time without having had an accident or without receiving any negative feedback. We must constantly remind ourselves of where we are, what we are doing and of the consequences of failure when we become too comfortable. Being uncomfortable challenges us and keeps us sharp. It helps us to keep our focus in the moment where it needs to be.

Sometimes people who were top performers in their field became too comfortable with very dangerous jobs. In their routine, they relaxed and lost their focus. They came out of their game and ultimately made mistakes that cost them their lives. While it is not likely that you will die from a bad presentation, it can be very difficult to regain the trust and confidence of an audience once you have lost it.

Remember that being uncomfortable is your friend. It sharpens your senses and keeps you focused on the task at hand. It is not something any of us need to run away from or avoid, we simply need to recognize the signs and learn to interpret what our discomfort is telling us. The better we become at understanding these subtle signs and indicators that our body sends out, the better we will be at accomplishing any task we set out to do. We must learn to function in the uncomfortable zone and pay close attention to the signals that our body is sending us. In this way, we can be safe and effective as we accomplish our goals. If we are going to achieve our goals in life, we must become comfortable being uncomfortable.

44

10—80—10 RULE OF PRESENTATION DEVELOPMENT

For those who must regularly prepare presentations this principle will help you to quickly and easily put together a presentation. Great presentations are made up of specific elements. If you know and understand the elements that go into a presentation, then you will be able to quickly identify what you need to add to your own presentation to produce a professional product. The 10-80-10 rule refers to the introduction, body and conclusion of a presentation; 10 percent is the introduction, 80 percent is the body and 10 percent is the conclusion. Each part of the presentation has components that are essential to making a presentation more effective and influential.

INTRODUCTION 10 %

-Start Strong
-Look Up and Lock In
-Theme Statement
-Quote
-What's In It For Me (WIIFM)

BODY 80 %

-Personal Anecdote
-Theme Repetition
-Supporting Data
-Rule of Three/Alliterations
-Develop Supporting Gestures
-Repeated Words and Phrases
-Show Passion
-X factor
-Self-deprecating Humor
-Examples
-Paint Word Pictures
-Visual Aids
-Conclusion Indicator

CONCLUSION 10%

—End Strong

-Slow down
-Call to Action
-Recap Theme
-Quote

Using this 10-80-10 outline, you can easily fill in the blanks and develop a presentation in a very short period of time that will look as though it was produced by a professional and will reflect the positive image that you want to project.

45

NEVER WRITE A PRESENTATION IN ADVANCE.

The mind is amazingly powerful but it's also very impressionable. Many people think that they are doing themselves a favor by writing down their presentation word for word and refining it over a period of time to produce a very well-thought-out, perfectly orchestrated presentation. The problem that we have here is the same problem we have when we write our notes in complete sentences. In our minds, if it is important enough to write, then it is important enough to read word for word and that is exactly what happens.

When a speaker stands before an audience, one of two things will happen. He is either going to try to give the presentation from memory or he is going to lose confidence in his memory and read the presentation. There are problems with both of these situations.

If we attempt to give a presentation from memory, we run the risk of forgetting something and few speakers are skilled enough to stay on track without going back to the written presentation, find their place and continue from there. Speakers will then become very flustered and frustrated with themselves, making it even harder to concentrate and remember what they memorized. This creates a demeanor shift that is very apparent to the audience. It tells the audience that this speaker is not sincere and that this is just a memorized and regurgitated presentation that is in no way coming from the heart of the speaker. At this point, the speaker will lose all credibility and influence with the audience. On the other hand, if we read our presentation, we evoke the exact same feelings and reaction from the audience because we are reading something that we did not feel was important enough to learn before we came to speak.

As speakers, we need to develop the mental flexibility to be able to say what we want to say in several different ways. We need to focus on the ideas rather than the words we want to use. By focusing on the ideas rather than the words, we maintain our cognitive focus in the present. We do not have to think about how to speak. This is a habitual process. All you need to remember is what you want to talk about and you will come up with the words in the moment to express yourself. Don't worry about trying to remember exactly how you said it when you practiced. The idea is to be able to express yourself and get your point across.

Remember, the audience does not know what you are going to say or how you are going to say it. So, as you give your presentation, if it does not come out exactly the way you wanted to express it, do not obsess over it. Only you will know and you can work on that later; but for now, be in the moment. Never write a presentation in advance.

46

PRACTICE ALLOWED

Although the mind is extremely powerful our bodies under stress are sometimes slow to respond to the mental image that we produce. Under stress, our bodies respond slowly and hesitantly until we develop muscle memory that replicates the mental picture we want to project. We may think, prior to being placed under stress, that we are going to do something but when we actually try to replicate that mental picture, our actions will be very restricted and small compared to what we think we are doing. This is because we have not developed our style of presentation.

For most of us, larger gestures and extreme vocal variation are not a part of our natural presentation style. Unlike experienced speakers who integrate these elements into their presentation as a part of their natural style, an inexperienced speaker must make these elements a part of his delivery plan, thinking about it ahead of time to ensure that he knows what he is going to do. Just to think to ourselves that we are going to be dynamic is not enough. What is dynamic? We must articulate exactly what we are going to do to bring life into our presentation.

Practicing out loud allows us to hear how we are going to sound as we give our presentation. Like any other process, it helps us to develop muscle memory as we are speaking. As we practice out loud, we pay particular attention to our voice inflections and the body language that we project as we are practicing. If a mirror is available, we should take advantage of practicing in front of it so that we can actually see our facial gestures and body language as we rehearse our presentation. Practicing a presentation is like practicing any physical skill. The more we can simulate the actual situation that we will experience as we practice, the more we will gain from the practice session.

There is a lot to be said for thinking a process through and using mental imagery. Few people, however, have the skill necessary to get the full benefit of just thinking through the process. They leave out too many details of the mental imagery process. They think of the words and leave out the vocal inflections and the body language as they focus on what they perceive as the most important and difficult part of the presentation. Although an experienced presenter may be able to do this because he has developed years of habits to support his technique, even he is more likely to practice his presentation aloud.

If you do not have a lot of experience with mental visualization, you may easily miss important aspects of the process. Just knowing the idea and remembering the key points of a presentation is only a small portion of the presentation itself. To get the full benefit, we must practice and develop our own individual style by acting it out and the best way to do this is to practice out loud.

47

AS CONFIDENCE GROWS, SPEAKING RATE SLOWS.

A common mistake of many speakers is that they talk too fast. In a state of heightened anxiety, they try to move through whatever is causing the anxiety as quickly as possible. Since public speaking causes high anxiety for most of us, we are in a hurry to try to get it over with, get off the stage and get out of a situation that is causing us so much tension.

The other reason that we speed up is that we are uncomfortable with silence or dead space and we feel that we must fill the silence by speaking faster. How much faster we speak is not as important as the fact that our speaking rate will increase. This works against us in two ways. One, it changes the rate at which we must process information. As we speak fast, we have to think faster. This may result in unnatural delays when we hit pauses and cannot remember what comes next because we are waiting for our thought process to catch up. When we practice, we develop a certain tempo that we get used to and when we change that tempo it throws off our rhythm.

The second problem is that speaking rapidly destroys the vocal variation of our presentation. As we speak faster and do not vary our pace we become monotone. This makes us sound as if we are droning rather than presenting to an audience, not to mention the effect this will have on the audience as they listen to such a presenter. They are getting a sense from that speaker as to how they should feel. If you are nervous and trying to move quickly through your material because you are anxious, this makes the audience anxious. They feel rushed and uncomfortable and are not relaxed and able to receive and interpret your message.

Seldom has a speaker been accused of speaking too slowly. Slowing down works for a presenter by providing time for him to think. Varying the pace of the presentation engages the attention of the audience. By slowing down, we pull the audience in; by varying the pace, we can emphasize the parts of our presentation that are important. We must get control of our rate of speech and deliver it at an optimum speed for the audience to receive and interpret the information. As confidence grows, speaking rate slows.

48

TO LIVE WITHOUT DISCIPLINE IS TO DIE WITHOUT DIGNITY.

Discipline is the key to all success. This is a bold statement and it is meant to be. Our nature in life is to take the easy or the comfortable way in everything we do. We are constantly seeking the path of least resistance in terms of personal comfort. Our success is constantly at odds with this internal desire but success is seldom found on the path of least resistance. Success is achieved when we set forth on a disciplined path of hard work and focused effort.

If success was easy, it would be found naturally by everyone because it is our nature to find the easy way to do things. Success is not easy, however, and because of this we have at our disposal a skill called discipline that we can train to work to our advantage as we drive forward in our pursuit of success. Discipline is a skill that can be developed and honed or it can be ignored. Like any muscle that is not used, it will get weak and atrophy. Discipline is a developed habitual process that some of us may be accustomed to using while for others, it is a skill that they do not have. Either way, it is important to understand that it is a skill that is learned and not just a choice that is made in a moment.

Many people think that they can just turn on their discipline activator like a light switch, choosing to apply it in some situations and not in others. This is not the case. Discipline is a habitual process that can be observed and tested for as a character trait that people have incorporated into their lives or they have not. What this means to us is that we do not have the luxury of picking and choosing where and when we want to act with discipline. It is an all or nothing trait. It's like saying that I am going to be a good golfer or a good parent today but not tomorrow. It just does not work like this. Discipline is not a choice but a state of being, a condition of our character. We cannot be disciplined in the big things and not be disciplined in the small things. It is a character trait that permeates every aspect of our life.

If we truly want to find success in life, we must first get control of ourselves and become disciplined so that we can apply it toward our goals. Part of getting control of our self discipline will include taking a look at every aspect of our life to determine if we are taking full advantage of the opportunities that are available to us. The only way to take advantage of these opportunities is through the application of discipline. To live without discipline is to die without dignity.

49

THE QUALITY OF A PERSON'S LIFE IS IN DIRECT PROPORTION TO THEIR COMMITMENT TO EXCELLENCE, REGARDLESS OF THEIR CHOSEN FIELD OF ENDEAVOR.

What is excellence? Why is it important to our lives? Does it really matter how we do something? Why does it matter?

Excellence is often defined as consistent superior performance. During our lifetime we will hear a lot about excellence. A great deal of attention is paid to those who are recognized as the top performers in any field from sports to business. What does this all mean to us in our everyday lives? For many people, the level of effort they put into their jobs has no impact on how much they get in return. The paycheck generally remains the same if they work hard or hardly work unless they work on commission. So, why is excellence important to us if it has no impact on the return we will receive? Excellence is not so much about being better than or making more than everyone else as much as it is about each of us living up to our own potential.

Excellence is another one of those character traits that says a lot about the individual. It is not a product of a single effort or quality that can be brought forward to produce superior results on demand. Performance quality is the result of a lot of small elements that come together to produce something greater than the sum of its parts. Life is like a movie reel with thousands of tiny frames or experiences that when played together produce a movie. If too many of the frames are flawed, the movie becomes distorted and may be defective, producing a less than excellent result. Our lives can be viewed the same way. We are not a reflection of a single snapshot or a single moment in our lives, but we are a resultant product of thousands of frames that when played together become a movie of our life.

So, what does the movie of your life look like? Are you late for work just a little too often or do you leave early a little more often than you should? Do you cut corners when you don't need to or put things off so that you can relax? Do you play a little too often? One of the greatest resources we have in life is time and we all have the same number of hours in a day. How you spend those hours is your choice. Do you spend your time striving to do things well in order to produce an excellent result, or do you spend your time trying to figure out how to get out of what needs to be done?

One of the interesting characteristics of the quest for excellence is that once we have started on that path, the process itself becomes habitual. When we take care of the small things in an excellent manner then we develop the habit of only doing things excellently. Do an assessment of your life and determine if excellence is a word that you would use to define your habits. The quality of a person's life is in direct proportion to their commitment to excellence, regardless of their chosen field of endeavor.

50

REPEAT WORDS AND PHRASES FOR EMPHASIS.

As speakers we have a responsibility to our audience. One of the key responsibilities is to let the audience know what is important and to offer them the help they need to remember it. There are many ways that a good communicator can do this and one of them is to repeat words and phrases. Great presentations are like a great song. They have a rhythm and a theme that is enjoyable and easy to follow. We want the audience to hum along with us as we are presenting our program. By developing a good chorus, we help our audience remember what is important and what needs to be remembered after the presentation is concluded.

Too many communicators use what I refer to as the bucket technique of presenting information. They load up a bucket with information and then they stand up before their audience and throw all of the information that is in the bucket up into the air over the heads of the audience and hope that they will get what they need. This is often the result of a lack of training and an understanding on the part of the speaker of what is important to the audience. It is a reflection of the speaker in one of two ways. Either it is an attempt by the speaker to show the audience how much he knows, or it is a way to take the focus off the presenter and redirect it onto the information. Either way it is not an effective way to influence an audience.

As we develop our theme throughout our presentation, we want to establish a 'chorus' that we repeat over and over to help the audience to remember what we are talking about. When we really want to make an important point, we will slow down and repeat words or phrases so that we get the audience's attention. Repetition breaks the normal pattern or flow of communications. When we do it, we heighten the attention of the audience, giving us an opportunity to make a point and put emphasis on what is important.

This should be part of your planning process when you are putting together your presentation. Unless you are a skilled professional speaker, this is not a natural process for you and it will need to be planned and practiced. It is not enough to assume that we are going to do it just because we want to. We each have habitual methods that we use to deliver presentations and until we make deliberate efforts to modify and change these processes we will always revert to our old patterns or methods under pressure. The next time you are putting together a presentation, determine where you want to put emphasis by repeating words and phrases that will draw the audience's attention to where you want them to focus. Great communicators repeat words and phrases for emphasis.

51

THERE IS NOTHING AS POWERFUL AS A WELL-PLACED PAUSE.

Many speakers are afraid of the 'dead space' or 'white space' in a presentation, those silent moments that occur from time to time resulting in great anxiety for the speaker. One of the elements of public speaking that many people have difficulty with is that they take responsibility for both sides of the conversation. Most of us are very comfortable with the process of daily two-way communications where each person is responsible for a portion of the conversation but not many people are comfortable with the idea of having to carry the entire conversation for any length of time. This is what public speaking is all about. For many speakers, this becomes problematic because they think they must not stop talking for any reason or it will appear as though they do not know what they are talking about or that they have made a mistake. Herein lies the problem. The audience is listening to our pattern of speech from the time we start talking. When we are nervous, we speak faster than normal so everything starts to run together. This monotonous, droning rhythm makes it very easy to recognize even the slightest change of pace and this change will represent a mistake on the part of the speaker.

The best thing we can do is to break up this pattern right from the start. By slowing down, we not only give ourselves a chance to think but we also give ourselves more opportunity to change our pace without alerting the audience to our mistakes. This puts our thinking more in line with the natural pace of our thought processes. By using this pattern, we have an opportunity to insert deliberate pauses to draw the audience in on the important points that we want to make. The attention of the audience might wander during a presentation but if the speaker stops speaking, this will instantly draw the attention of the entire audience directly to the speaker. What happened? Why did it just get quiet? Why don't I hear anyone talking? At that moment, they all look up to find out what changed and then you have them. This is the moment when you have drawn all eyes to you and now is the time to make your point. Now the audience cannot miss it because you have demanded their attention with your silence. For the people who already have been paying

all eyes to you and now is the time to make your point. Now the attention, it gives them a moment to process what you have said and helps to develop an anticipation of what is going to come next.

Deliberate pauses are a powerful tool that can be used to draw in an audience. To use this effectively, speakers must first learn not to be afraid of the dead space or silence in their presentations. There is nothing more powerful than a well-placed pause.

52

SHARE PERSONAL ANECDOTES.

In order to make a connection and influence an audience we must first develop a relationship with them. Audiences do not naturally buy into statistics. Statistics may or may not stimulate a feeling depending on how closely they are connected to situations that the audience is emotionally tied in with. To be influential we must develop a relationship with our audience. We all have feelings about people and their feelings will in large part determine how an audience receives the information or statistics that are being presented. So, rather than trying to hide from the audience behind a wall of statistics and data, presenters need to work hard at developing a relationship with their audience.

There are many tools that we have at our disposal to accomplish this and one of the most powerful is the personal anecdote. We want the audience to get to know us and one way to do this is by sharing some things about ourselves. Again, this would not be just statistical data but would be a story about ourselves that gives the audience some insight into who we are and where we come from. A good speaker develops what I refer to as a quid pro quo with the audience. If we want the audience to lower their defenses and be receptive to what we are presenting, then we have to be willing to open up and share a little bit about ourselves. Once we share some of our own vulnerabilities and frailties, we become more like them in their eyes rather than being seen as just another con man or manipulator.

Once the audience sees a presenter as a person and not as a boss, a teacher, or a salesperson, they are much more open to being touched on a personal level. Many people are afraid to share their mistakes or frailties with others because they are afraid that people will think less of them. The truth is that it takes a very strong person to be able to share his or her weaknesses with others, but knowing that they have risen above these weaknesses empowers them to share their stories. There is a real strength in this that the audience can see and as we share our stories, they will begin to see a bit of themselves in us.

As humans, we all have a story to tell. Take some time to develop your story so that the next time you are giving a presentation you can share a personal anecdote.

53

DIRECTIONALITY WITH FLEXIBILITY

Great speakers have directionality with flexibility. This is a skill that may take some time to develop because it requires a bit of a repertoire to draw from but it is the mark of a skilled communicator. As presenters, we want to develop the skill of talking about ideas rather than from pre-developed sentences. This is why scripted presentations can be very cumbersome and problematic for speakers who have not already developed considerable skills.

One of the primary components that allow us to connect with an audience is speaking with passion, from the heart, and nothing will take the power out of a presentation more than reading or attempting to recite from memory. Audiences connect and get involved with the passion of the speaker, but if a speaker is just working from a memorized or transcripted presentation, his audience will perceive it as not personal.

There are many things that can distract us during a presentation and pull us away from our original plan. If we are paying close attention to the audience, they will indicate to us when we are on track with them and when we are not. Their interest, questions and curiosity can be your guide as you move through your presentation. The key will be for you to not lose sight of where you want to take the audience.

As influencers, we want to hold the attention of the audience by paying attention to what interests them, but we need not allow their interest to keep us from getting to our ultimate goal. As we prepare our presentation, one of the first things we need to determine is what we are trying to accomplish. This could include teaching, persuading, entertaining, convincing, informing, leading, selling or any combination of these. These are our objectives and as we move through our presentation we must always keep the objective in mind.

The next thing we must do is develop key topics that will act as markers on our path as we move toward our objective. The key topics will help to keep us from getting too far off track. Memorized or transcripted presentations do not have the flexibility necessary to move with the audience. In developing a presentation, an effective speaker will want to maintain directionality with flexibility to move the audience on a journey of discovery.

54

USE QUOTES.

Quotes are wonderful tools that we have at our disposal as we develop our presentations. Quotes work for us in multiple ways. One of the first things a quote does for us is that it gives us the appearance of being educated or well-versed on the topic. A speaker once said that he found people always believed him just a little bit more when he started his presentation with "Thomas Edison once said . . . ."

In using judicious and appropriate quotes, we are drawing a line connecting the person being quoted with our own ideas. We are creating credibility by association. After all, if it was good enough for Thomas Edison then it must be good enough for us. Right?

Another positive aspect of using quotes is that it shows the audience we have done our homework and we are prepared. It lets the audience know that what is being presented is a well thought-out and researched presentation and not just something being tossed out off-the-cuff. There is nothing worse than listening to a speaker who has not put his thoughts together or has not done his research to get the facts and data necessary to support his presentation. This is perceived negatively by the audience and the speaker loses all credibility.

Quotes also provide us with an appropriate catchphrase for our presentation. Repeating the phrase gives us an opportunity to introduce a theme to work with as we are developing our presentation.

Quotes are a great asset and they can come from many sources; they don't have to be just quotes from famous persons. Quotes can be words of wisdom that our parents used as we were growing up or personal quotes that we have come up with ourselves. There are many sources for finding quotes, including the internet and the library which houses numerous books full of quotes. These are often listed by topics or attributed to specific individuals. Regardless of where the quotes come from, they add a great dimension to any presentation. Sometimes the quote can simply provide a great segue for a speaker to talk about a particular character or a period of time. It may or may not have direct relevance to his topic but it can provide the flexibility needed to transition to different topics.

As powerful as quotes can be, they are double-edged swords that can hurt a speaker as well. It might be tempting to use too many quotes. This would have the same result as using statistics to hide behind. The other danger of quotes is that they may not be presented well. When you want to use a quote, use it powerfully. Great speakers don't say things like "I have a quote I want to share." "There is a quote that I like to use." Great speakers take ownership of any quote they use. They repeat it as if it is their driving philosophy rather than just some random saying that may or may not be related to the topic at hand.

Try to use quotes that you can present without reading. Reading quotes detracts from their power much the same as reading any part of a presentation. The next time you are putting together a presentation, find one or two applicable quotes that will support your presentation and draw the audience in. To ensure that your presentation is 'sticky', use quotes.

55

USE ALLITERATIONS.

As a speaker, I am responsible for what the audience remembers and does not remember about any presentation that I give. Because of this, I must work diligently to apply every tool at my disposal to ensure that the audience takes away all that I want them to take away. I know from years of experience that what I say may be important, but what the audience remembers is even more important. This will be determined not only by what I say but also how I say it. In addition to ensuring that my presentation appeals to auditory, visual and kinesthetic learning styles, I want to pay particular attention to learning aids that I can develop that will help the audience to remember what I want them to remember. One of these tools is the use of alliterations.

Alliteration is a series of words that begin with the same letter. For example: Confidence, Competence and Character or Verbal, Vocal and Visual. By developing alliterations, I make it easy for my audience to remember what I want them to remember because every word will start with the same letter. This is something that must be put together during the content phase of our presentation development. By taking the time to do this, I help to organize my presentation and develop key words that will not only help the audience to remember what I say but it will also help me to remember what I want to say.

This process forces us to organize our information in a logical and easy-to-remember format that can be readily grasped and easily recalled. Alliteration, the rule of three, personal stories and repeated words and phrases are all designed to ensure that our audience gets exactly what we want them to get. If for some reason they do not, it is probably because we have failed as communicators to present the information in a manner that allows our audience to easily recall the data.

It is not enough to just throw a lot of information at an audience and hope they get what we want them to get. We must take the time to understand that every individual is different and the more we use the various tools available to us, the more likely it is that we will be effective in our communications process. The next time you are putting together a presentation, take the time to develop some alliterations. You and your audience will be glad you did.

56

MAKE THE PRESENTATION STICKY.

We live in an information age where many people are overloaded with information. We receive much more information in a day than we could possibly remember. As communicators, it is incumbent upon us to design our information in such a manner that it helps people to remember it. That is what all of this is about. All the principles presented in this book are designed to use the verbal, vocal, and visual elements of communication to their absolute maximum potential. There are very few things that people hear in a day that are unique enough to stand out, let alone motivate action. There is a huge advertising industry designed to drive our actions every day and we are bombarded with ads and information, the purpose of which is to drive us toward particular actions. The information is driving us to make a buy, realize a vision, or to apply something new in our lives.

As communicators, we are doing the same thing and it is easy to get lost in a sea of other communicators if we are not careful. How do we stand out? What do we do that is different? What makes our presentation memorable? These are the question that we must ask ourselves. We must always remember that when we are making a presentation, it is probably not the first time that the audience has heard some of this information and most likely, it will not be the last.

When people are ready to receive and when they are ready to take action upon what a communicator has to say is often a matter of timing. As an example, most of us receive hundreds of communications per week attempting to get us to apply for another credit card, work with another investment firm, use another realtor, change our insurance, take out a loan, buy products on sale, eat at particular restaurants, buy a particular car and many other things. This information is coming at us many times per week because whatever action we choose to take will be in large part a matter of which ad arrived in the mailbox at a particular time.

This is the same problem we run into as communicators. We may not be saying anything that the audience has not heard before so how do we differentiate our product or presentation in such a manner that we will be remembered? How do we stand out in a sea of information that our audience is flooded with every day? Making our presentation 'sticky' is about being remembered. It is about standing out from the crowd so that when someone does want to remember what was said, it helps them to recall it by remembering the person who said it. As communicators, we always have to remember that it is not what we say that matters most but what the audience takes away. A speaker can make the best presentation in the world but if the audience does not remember any of it, it will not be effective in the long run. If we want to be remembered and we want our information to be helpful, we must make our presentation 'sticky' so that the audience will remember us long after our program ends.

57

GIVE THE AUDIENCE A CONCLUSION INDICATOR.

There are two characteristics of an audience that we must always keep in mind as we are preparing and presenting a presentation. First of all, audiences are very easily distracted and second, they are very time conscious. We all have a peak period where we are able to pay attention to what is going on and after that we begin to lose our focus. This is why many employers rotate their people to several different job positions throughout the day. By changing positions, employees are forced to refocus their attention to the task at hand keeping them sharp.

For a presenter this is very difficult to do. The attention span of an audience is like an upside-down bell curve. At the beginning of a presentation, the audience is very focused on what is being said; as the presentation continues, the audience becomes less and less focused on what the speaker is saying and begins to drift. By the conclusion of a presentation, the audience begins to refocus in the moment and prepares to leave and move on to their next task. Knowing all this allows the presenter to get his information out to the audience during a time when their attention is at a peak focus, during the moments at the beginning and at the end of the presentation.

As we prepare to move into our conclusion or the last 10 percent of our presentation, we can bring the audience back into the moment by letting them know that we are preparing to wrap everything up and put a bow on it for them. We do this with a conclusion indicator. We simply tell the audience that we are almost done. There are many examples of how to do this and here are just a few: 1. As we wrap this up today. 2. If you don't remember anything else I have said today, this is what you want to take away. 3. As I draw this presentation to a close, I ask you to remember just a few things.

When we use this language we are telling the audience that we are preparing to wrap up. Now is the time to give them the takeaway that you have prepared for them. At this point, you will have the audience's peak attention so it is important to be very clear and concise on exactly what you want them to remember. This is where the second characteristic of an audience's time consciousness plays a crucial role. If we give a conclusion indicator, we better be concluding. Many an untrained speaker has lost all credibility by giving a conclusion indicator and then just repeating everything he has already said. This is not the time to attempt to restate everything that you have just said during the body of your presentation. This would be far too much information and you will lose the attention of the audience as well as your credibility.

As a final point, this is the time to make a personal connection with the audience. Try not to look at your notes during the conclusion. This is where you can build that lasting rapport that will make you and your presentation memorable to your audience. In order to ensure that your presentation has the maximum impact, give the audience a conclusion indicator and then conclude.

58

LESS THAN 10 PERCENT OF OUR NERVOUSNESS TRANSMITS TO THE AUDIENCE.

One of the most difficult things for any speaker to do is to understand what the audience sees in us. This is one of the reasons that professional coaching is invaluable for any speaker in the development of a presentation. Specific feedback is an essential tool in the development of any skill and it is hard to come by in the real world. Most presentations will result in a limited amount of non-specific feedback from the audience such as thank you, good job, well done, that was great, etc. This is always nice to hear and it may make us feel good, but it is hardly what we need if we are to grow and develop our skills as a speaker.

There are three reasons why this type of limited feedback is problematic. One is that it is not specific and it gives the speaker nothing to work with. It does not tell us what was good or what was not good. It does not give us ideas on what we can do better or what we need to work on to make our presentation more effective in the future.

Two, the nonspecific feedback is not necessarily true. Most people want to be polite and so regardless of how poorly you do in your presentation, you are going to receive praise from some of the audience simply in recognition of your effort.

The third problem is that it is unlikely that members of your audience are trained to recognize the specific elements that actually will enhance your presentation. This then becomes a situation of the blind leading the blind. When you receive feedback you have to look at the source and ask yourself if the individual providing it has sufficient skills or knowledge to provide feedback that you are willing to accept and incorporate into your presentation.

Most nonprofessional speakers feel a certain nervousness or anxiety as they step up onto the stage. Inside, they are scared to death and they think that the rest of the world, or at least their audience can sense this. Audiences only know what a presenter shows them and this is why actions as well as words are so important. Audiences do not want to be uncomfortable so they are looking to the speaker to relax them. If the speaker is nervous or scared, the audience will be also. No audience wants to watch a speaker impale himself upon his own words. It is like watching a horrific crash in slow motion. There is a tremendous amount of anxiety that builds up as we watch in dread, hoping that the speaker does not embarrass himself.

Most of the struggle that is going on inside of us is the result of the unknown. We do not know what we look like so we are worried about what the audience will think of us. It is like painting a picture in the dark and then not having an opportunity to see it before it is presented to an audience. At that moment, the only knowledge we will have about the quality of our presentation will be based on the feedback from the audience. This would scare the heck out of anyone. As speakers we must always remember that less than 10 percent of our nervousness is projected to the audience. As long as we can control the shaking of our hands and the stammer in our voice, the audience is not likely to notice that we are scared to death.

Professional coaches use video cameras to record presentations so that clients can see exactly what the audience is seeing. This gives the presenter a look at his painting before the audience sees it, allowing him an opportunity to make corrections before he has to stand in front of the audience. This is what makes video feedback so valuable as a training tool. It is a glimpse into what the audience is going to see and that empowers us as speakers. In order to recognize our potential, we must always remember that less than 10 percent of our nervousness transmits to our audience.

59

OUR ATTITUDE, NOT OUR APTITUDE, DETERMINES OUR ALTITUDE.

We have all heard it before. Attitude is everything! Why is this so? What makes attitude so powerful? It is the one thing that we have complete control over in every aspect of our life. We may not be able to have any impact on events that occur around us but we certainly have complete control over how we perceive those events. Our perception of events will subsequently drive how we use our knowledge to respond to situations and how we arrive at the various choices that we develop.

Knowledge is filtered through the lens of our attitude. Attitude is the driving force behind knowledge. If we perceive the options available to us as poor, then that is how we will treat them. If, however, we perceive those options as good opportunities, then we will treat them that way.

Knowing the difficulties involved does not always make any job easier but it is how we perceive these obstacles that will determine the difficulty of the job. For many people, obstacles are an opportunity to excel while for others obstacles are a reason to quit. A willingness to strive and do your best in the face of adversity, regardless of the difficulty, is what attitude is all about.

Attitude is the reflection of the spirit of the individual. When we hear that a person has a great spirit, we know that the person has a great attitude. We love to be around people like this. They empower their friends and colleagues and make them feel as though anything is possible. Thinkers may know how to do it but people with spirit are the people who get the job done. There are many educated idiots in the world and a lot of educated people who never come anywhere near achieving their potential in life.

Attitude is what drives us in the face of all of the naysayers and negativity that each of us will face as we move toward our goals in life. Attitude is our best defense against all of the things that people tell us cannot be done or should not be done in life. President John F. Kennedy's attitude was reflected in his speech about going to the moon. There were many people who thought that going to the moon was a waste of money or just an ego trip to beat the Russians because it served no purpose. But look at the knowledge and inventions that came from that landmark event. Things that had never before been imagined had to be made from scratch in order to accomplish the monumental task of reaching the moon. It was not just knowledge that made this possible, but attitude. The attitude that said, even though it hasn't been done, it doesn't mean that I can't do it. The attitude that said, even though the technology does not yet exist, it doesn't mean that I can't make it. The attitude that said, if it is to be, it is up to me.

Attitude is what gets things done. Knowledge is just a tool sitting on a shelf waiting to be used until attitude comes along and puts action to it. Our attitude, not our aptitude, determines our altitude.

60

TAKE RISKS

We have become a risk-averse society that has developed a phobia of failure. Our life motto has changed from "It is better to have tried and failed than never to have tried at all." to "It is better not to even try if there is even the slightest chance of failure."

Success and failure, like winning and losing, come with inherent risk. As soon as we set a goal and state it so that others know that this is our intent, we have taken on a risk. The setting of goals, or any objective for that matter, carries with it a possibility of success and a possibility of failure as well. This is the risk.

There is good news, however. Risk is a part of anything we choose to do in our lives. We need failures in our lives just as we need success. We are driven by and learn far more from our failures than we do from our successes.

Risk comes in two distinct forms. There is the risk that is associated with the success and failure of the task and there is the risk that is associated with the impact that failure will have on us psychologically. How we deal with the psychological impact of failure is far more important than the actual failure of the project. The success or failure of a project can be evaluated mathematically in most instances. The difficulty arises when we tie the two together by attaching our attitude to the outcome of a goal.

Our attitude toward failure is a key component to determining our future. We have all heard the story about how Thomas Edison responded when asked if he got discouraged after so many failed experiments when he was trying to identify a material that would work as a filament for the light bulb. Thomas Edison proclaimed that he had never failed. Every time something didn't work, he had learned of one more material that would not work. That was not a failure.

Edison's attitude never changed. It was not associated with the outcome of an event but was the product of a vision that was inside the man and could not be altered. Failure is a possible outcome in everything we do in life, in every risk we take. The key is to not let failure have a negative impact on attitude. Perhaps it is as simple as the terminology that we use to describe circumstances in our lives. The language that we use often determines how we feel about things. A negative result can be labeled a 'failure' or it can be seen as a 'learning opportunity'. This is often determined by the expectation that we have as we go into a situation.

Having a negative attitude can have a major impact on our perspective of a situation. For example, if we enter a classroom thinking that we know a lot about a topic and the professor shows us that we do not, we might develop a negative attitude toward the professor. This view of the professor will then have an impact on how we receive information from him in the future. Life is an adventure and if we are going to experience that adventure to the fullest, we must become comfortable with risk. This does not mean that we are going to be haphazard in our work and irresponsible in our attitude but that we are not going to avoid doing something just because we fear the negative psychological impact that failure will have on us. In order to experience the great victories that are waiting for us out there, we must become comfortable taking risk.

61

FOUR TYPES OF PRESENTATIONS

There are four types of presentations that we can give. We must know and understand the strengths and weaknesses of each in order to use them to their fullest potential when we are trying to influence an audience. As we are preparing a presentation, there are times when each one of these four types of presentations might be utilized. If one is used inappropriately in the place of another, it can have a devastating impact upon the effectiveness of the presentation or influence that the speaker intended to have on the audience. Manuscript, memorized, extemporaneous and impromptu are each a type of presentation that has its place. As speakers, we must choose wisely the best one to use based on the information and the audience.

Manuscript is a written presentation that is intended to be read. Reading destroys 90 percent of our presentation's effectiveness because it eliminates our ability to develop a rapport with the audience. So why do we need manuscripts? There are times when speakers cannot stand up and speak for themselves. I have seen this at business functions and college graduations where the guest speaker was unable to attend but did have a message that he wanted to share with the audience. In these instances, the speaker who was unable to attend provided a manuscript to someone whom he felt could represent him in reading his words. The key in this situation is to keep it brief. Most audiences will understand this situation and will be more tolerant of a read presentation as long as it does not get too long-winded. If the reading goes on for more than five minutes, then the audience will begin to get uncomfortable, distracted and disinterested.

Memorized presentations can help the speaker or hurt the speaker depending on the level of skill the speaker possesses. For the untrained speaker, a memorized presentation can cause more problems than it can provide solutions. When attempting to deliver a presentation from memory, if the speaker forgets where he is or needs to refer to his notes, it becomes immediately apparent to the audience that this is a memorized presentation. Finding the place where he got lost can be a very difficult and cumbersome process for the speaker. The break in flow and style signals to the audience that maybe the speaker was trying to trick them and they now have seen through the ruse. For a trained professional with the flexibility to flow smoothly from one topic group to another, memorizing has a place. Memorizing some audience-specific information can provide the opportunity to tailor a presentation for the audience. If we have the ability to flow and are not constrained by the exact words that are associated with the topics, we are more comfortable and confident as we speak.

Extemporaneous is the most versatile and preferred of the four presentation styles. This is the process of having an outline that we speak to but we present from the heart using our personal style. This is the best way to make a connection with the audience. We take the concentrated focus off the words and put them on the topic areas that we want to cover. This method gives us perfect directionality with flexibility. This is where we should all aspire to be in our presentation styles.

The last type of presentation is the impromptu. This is speaking off-the-cuff on the spur of the moment, generally with little or no warning. For most people this is the most difficult because they have not had time to prepare. There are two tips that will help here. One, keep it short and don't feel as though you have to speak all night. Three or four minutes is fine. Two, talk about what you want to talk about, what you know. Have some way to turn your presentation into something that you are familiar with and talk to that topic in an extemporaneous manner.

This is one reason I always encourage presenters to develop three or four stump speeches with quotes to support the message. A stump speech involves a topic important to you that you can talk about for four or five minutes, one that you have already prepared and have thought through so that you are never caught off guard. Being able to give one of these presentations with little or no warning will significantly enhance your overall credibility. Knowing when and where to apply the four different types of presentation will work to your advantage.

62

NEVER TURN YOUR BACK ON THE AUDIENCE.

This may sound simplistic but as we develop as speakers, it becomes more of an issue. The more comfortable we are as speakers, the more dynamic we become. This leads to movement into and amongst the audience. This is good because it helps us to develop a rapport with the audience. Distance is a barrier that is very difficult to overcome if we do not have control over our environment. The problem arises when we have a somewhat untraditional stage or no stage at all. Theaters-in-the-round or the unconventional setting of a large living room can present particular problems as we move into the audience to close the distance with individuals. At this point, by the nature of the setting, we have our back to some people while facing others. As speakers, we must learn to move slowly and smoothly as we navigate through a maze of people in an attempt to eliminate the barrier of distance between speaker and audience. In some situations, we must simply adapt to our surroundings and do the best we can.

If we do have control, then we need to be aware of what works best for us and how we can take advantage of our environment to have the greatest influence with our audience. As we practice moving in and out of our audience, we must be careful not to turn our backs on them as we move back toward the front of the group. We can do this by smoothly walking backwards or turning to talk to other audience members while continuing to move toward the front. The challenge is less about not turning our backs than it is about addressing the audience while we are moving. If we are making eye contact and talking as we are moving, then we are still connected and that, of course, is our goal. We do not want to lose the connection that we have developed with the audience.

We must practice turning our bodies and talking to people as we move. Some speakers may develop a pattern of looking over their shoulders as they are talking to people on their left and right rather than turning their entire body and squaring off and addressing them directly. The eye contact is important but the body position is important as well. By looking at someone over our shoulder we are acknowledging their presence with our eye contact but we are not recognizing them as individuals who deserve our full attention. A speaker who talks to people by simply looking over his shoulder at them is not giving them the attention or respect that they deserve. Although consciously an audience might recognize conditions of the environment, their subconscious is going to wonder if the speaker does not think they are important enough to turn and recognize them. As you are developing your presentation, take into consideration your movements. Make sure that you move in such a way that you do not turn your back on any part of the audience.

63

AUDIENCES LOVE HUMOR, ESPECIALLY SELF-DEPRECATING HUMOR.

We must learn to have fun and not take ourselves too seriously if we want the audience to take us seriously. The first thing that most speakers think of when we tell them to use humor in their presentation is a comedian who stands up on stage and makes us laugh for hours. Most of us are not trying to be comedians but simply attempting to make a connection with the audience.

Humor does a lot of things for us. The act of smiling produces hormones in our body that relax us as we are preparing to do something stressful. This is important for the audience and speaker alike.

Also humor allows the audience and the speaker to agree on something and that sets the tone and launches a trend of agreement. This can be very powerful for any speaker attempting to influence an audience. Finding a common ground through humor enables us to begin the journey of discovery from the same place.

Humor comes in many forms and some people are better with it than others. Like so many things in communications, humor can be a doubled-edged sword. If we try to employ humor and it falls flat, this can have a negative impact on the audience. There are many conditions that determine whether the humor that we employ will be effective. Culture, age, background, knowledge, and interest are all conditions that can limit the effectiveness of humor. Knowing how and when to use it is as important as knowing what to say. The real difficulty of a joke is that it is so audience-dependent. A great joke told well with the wrong audience can cause more problems than a poor joke poorly told to the right audience. Because many jokes can insult or offend, speakers must be very careful in their choice of what humor to use with specific audiences.

Humor is a very powerful tool but it is a dangerous tool as well so one of the things we recommend is the use of self-deprecating humor. We can reduce this risk of insulting or offending others by making fun of ourselves. In having a little fun with ourselves we do two things. First, it helps us to connect because it demonstrates to the audience that we are confident enough to share something personal about ourselves by using humor. The second thing it does is show that the speaker is human with strengths and weaknesses just like everyone in the audience. This is a great connection to make because it personalizes a speaker to an audience.

Audiences love to laugh and we, as speakers and entertainers love to make people laugh. One of the safest ways to do this is to make fun of ourselves. Next time you are putting together a presentation, remember that audiences love humor, especially self-deprecating humor.

64

TO ELIMINATE FILLERS, WE MUST IMPLEMENT "STS".

Most speakers are very uncomfortable with the deafening quiet that comes rushing in as soon as they stop talking for a split second. All speakers develop a natural speaking pattern and when they are nervous that pattern changes. For most of us, this means an increase in the rate of speech. This works against us in two ways. First, our speaking rate is generally faster than our normal thinking rate so now our thinking and our words are out of sync causing our delivery to become very jerky. In order to appear smoother, we fill in the resulting holes with fillers. Fillers can be words or non-words used in a repetitive pattern to fill in what should have been a silent space providing an opportunity for the speaker to think about what he is going to say next. 'And', 'ah', 'ya know', 'umm', 'okay', 'all right', 'an' are all examples of fillers that speakers use to offset silence. These are often called transitional fillers as they are used by the speaker as a means to flow or transition from one sentence to another without actually having to stop talking.

There is nothing that demonstrates the inexperience of a speaker like the use of fillers. One of the intriguing things about fillers is that an untrained speaker may use them liberally and naturally but unknowingly. When asked about this after a presentation, the speaker often will deny having used them at all. This is another good reason why professional coaching is so important to anyone who has to communicate for a living.

Speakers need not only to see what the audience sees but they need to hear what the audience hears as well. Once a speaker becomes aware that he is using fillers, he can eliminate the habit fairly easily by implementing STS. This is a simple process of coming to the end of a thought and taking time to Stop, Think and Speak (STS). This momentary hesitation gives the speaker's brain a moment to catch up with his words, allowing him to move smoothly into his next thought without the need for transitional fillers.

Another thing that speakers must be careful to avoid is seeking approval from the audience. We must be confident in what we are saying with or without feedback from the audience. Seeking approval can make a speaker appear as though he does not believe what he is saying so he is trying to convince himself by convincing his audience. Words and phrases such as 'okay', 'all right', 'you know', 'you know what I mean', 'do you get it?' are all a speakers attempt to gain approval from the audience. This not only makes the speaker appear desperate but it also can seem as though the speaker considers the audience slow because they are not grasping the information. This is a surefire way for any speaker to lose connection with an audience. Do not attempt to seek approval from the audience. Be confident in what you are saying and let the people in the audience come to their own conclusions. All we have to do to eliminate fillers is to implement STS.

65

IF I TALK TO EVERYONE, I COMMUNICATE WITH NO ONE; IF I TALK TO ONE PERSON, I WILL COMMUNICATE WITH EVERYONE.

Why is it so much more difficult to talk to a group of people than it is to talk to one person? One of the main differences that comes immediately to mind is that when we give a presentation to a group it generally becomes a monologue rather than a dialogue. This simply means that the speaker is doing all the talking. So we prepare for hours and hours to ensure that we are able to carry the conversation.

Another thing that public speakers must deal with is how to view an audience. As we are presenting our information we have a tendency to view the audience as one object, one audience. Subconsciously, this may be easier to deal with; rather than thinking of the tens, hundreds or thousands of individuals in the group, we lump them into one mass. In an attempt to talk to this unwieldy beast with so many eyes and so many ears, some speakers may become confused, not knowing which ears to talk to and which eyes to look at. In their confusion, they often gaze out over the audience with darting eyes, trying to talk to everyone at the same time. Or they may pick a spot on the wall in the back of the room and not even attempt to make eye contact with the audience. In the worst case scenarios, nervous speakers may revert back to looking down and reading their thoroughly memorized, well-rehearsed presentation to avoid any eye contact at all with the audience.

The key is to not lump the audience together as one mass of people, but to see them as individuals that you need to connect with. Each and every one of them has a need to hear your message. The best way for you to ensure that they receive from you the attention they need is for you to see your audience as the individuals they are. So as you are preparing to give your presentation, practice looking up, locking in, and speaking to one person. As you move your eyes slowly across the audience and lock in with individuals for three to five seconds, you will gain the advantage by means of something called the aurora effect. This basically means that as you are looking at one person, many others sitting around that person will believe you are looking directly at them. The farther away they are from the speaker, the more people in that area believe he is looking at them.

Remember that it is less important what you do than how the audience perceives what you do. While you may be looking at only a few people in the audience, many others will feel as though you are looking at each of them. The next time you are preparing for a presentation, remember to see the audience as individuals rather than as one mass of bodies. When we talk to everyone, we communicate with no one but when we talk to one person, we communicate with everyone. If you can remember this, the beast with many eyes and many ears will seem much more manageable.

66

RULE OF THREE

As speakers we want our audience to remember the information we are presenting so we must put that information in a format that will allow it to be easily remembered. In preparing our information for delivery, we want to give the audience takeaways that can be referred to at a later date. It does not so much matter what we say as a speaker, it only matters what the audience remembers. We must be careful not to overload our audience with information. Although audiences may be smart, they have a limited capacity to remember lists of information or statistics. The brain is basically lazy unless the information being presented is of particular importance or interest to cause the data to be committed to memory. Audiences will not generally take the time to develop memory keys to help them recall information being presented. This responsibility falls to the presenter. Most people can easily recall three items when they hear them in a presentation. If they are presented with four items in a presentation, they will generally remember three, forgetting one of the two in the middle.

There are many examples of how the concept of three is used in our society. From the time we are born we hear it in our nursery rhymes and fairy tales telling the stories of three blind mice or the three little pigs. In religion it is the Holy Trinity and the three wise men while sports give us the triple threat, triple point and the Triple Crown. Three is a number that is easy to work with which is why our phone numbers and social security numbers both start with three numbers. We are a society that lumps things into groups of three to make it easier for us to remember.

As you are preparing your presentation, try to come up with three things that you want the audience to take away. Present these three things repeatedly throughout your presentation. This continual referral to the three things that you want to 'stick' will help your listeners to remember the key points, the takeaway, that you want the audience to remember long after they leave the presentation. This is part of making the presentation 'sticky' so that it is not easily forgotten.

The concept of three can work as an outline as well, allowing your presentation to flow smoothly and making it easier for you to recall what is next. The next time you are preparing a presentation, do yourself and your audience a favor. Come up with a rule of three that you can use to make your presentation more memorable and give the audience a 'sticky' takeaway.

67

CALL PEOPLE OUT BY NAME.

There is no sweeter sound to the human ear than the sound of one's own name. For a presenter, being able to call on people by name is a very powerful tool. Establishing rapport with an audience can provide instant credibility for the speaker. Referring to people by name so that everyone else knows that you have a relationship with them is a great foot in the door when you are making first contact with an audience that is unfamiliar with you or your program. Just the mere mention of people who are known to and respected by the audience can give the speaker a certain degree of credibility.

The second thing that mentioning people by name does for a speaker is that it commands the attention of the audience. Mentioning people by name makes the point that the speaker might call upon anyone in the audience for a comment so the entire audience must be prepared. This degree of uncertainty forces the audience to stay tuned into the presentation so that they do not get caught off guard.

The last thing that calling people by name does is that it makes those people feel special. It is gratifying to be recognized and remembered; and when we feel that the speaker has taken the time to do this, it makes us feel good about ourselves and about the speaker by association. Whenever a speaker can be associated with good feelings that people have about themselves his credibility is enhanced in their eyes.

Like everything else, this potentially valuable tool can be a double-edged sword. In calling people by name we need to be careful about what kind of interaction we develop with the audience. If we choose to ask questions, for example, we may want to ask only open-ended questions, questions for which there are no right or wrong answers. These can come in the form of fact-finding questions or questions seeking an opinion. We do this because we do not want to embarrass people in our audience. If we embarrass people in the audience, it scares others and makes them resent the speaker who makes them feel insecure. It is a sure way for a speaker to alienate himself from an audience.

Speakers should be careful about using answers from an audience to help guide their presentation. I have seen presenters design a presentation based on the responses that they intend to solicit from the audience and then find themselves forced to spend a great deal of time trying to coax the answers they need out of the audience. Finally, in desperation, they just give the audience the answer. This can be very clumsy and gives the audience a lot of control over your presentation. If you develop a dialogue with the audience, you must constantly maintain control and keep your presentation on track in terms of timing and material. The next time you want to gain credibility with an audience, call on some of the people in the audience by name.

68

DON'T TELL THE AUDIENCE WHAT YOU ARE GOING TO DO OR SAY, JUST DO OR SAY IT.

There is nothing more irritating to an audience than feeling as if they are being talked down to or are being spoon-fed by a presenter. As presenters we become our greatest asset and our worst enemy at the same time. Many speakers, suck the life right out of their presentations, removing all the surprise and power, by giving the audience all the answers before they even ask any questions. Great communicators know how to develop interest and anticipation in their presentations. They keep us on the edge of our seats wanting more. A skilled communicator can motivate us to formulate a question in our minds and then dangle the answer in front of us until we just about cannot stand it any more. Then, at just the right moment, he will hit us right between the eyes with it.

Skilled communicators make the experience exciting for an audience, taking them to places they never expected to see. Just when they begin to wonder what they are doing here, the speaker lifts the veil and all is revealed in a moment of clarity, giving the audience a greater understanding not only of the topic but the entire experience as well.

Many people have heard the old saying about telling the audience what you want to tell them, then tell them, and then tell them what you told them. There is nothing wrong with this as long as you understand that there are different types of journeys. It can be a journey in your car from your house to the local grocery store or it can be a journey on a motorcycle through the great Rocky Mountains. They are both journeys but they have nothing in common other than movement. Sometimes a speaker is so worried about being misunderstood that he tries to be overly clear and too literal. In an effort to not be misunderstood, he explains every detail of what he is doing and saying.

This often happens when people try to use quotes. Many speakers need to preface the quote with a statement like: I want to share a quote with you today or I have a quote here that I think relates to what I want to talk about. It is as if he is afraid that the audience will not recognize it is a quote when he delivers it. Audiences are pretty smart and we need to give them some credit. Simply starting with "Thomas Jefferson once said

. . ." or, "It is said that . . ." gives the audience all the explanation needed. Better yet, skip the introduction and just give the quote as though it is yours and then give credit at the end. We command the attention of the audience more when we take command of our words and own them. Don't suck the life out of your presentation by telling your audience what you are going to do or say. Just do it or say it.

69

ARISTOTLE'S THREE COMPONENTS OF COMMUNICATIONS.

Communications has been recognized throughout history as a skill needed to move society. Aristotle was one of the great teachers of his day and he spent a great deal of time thinking about what it took to be a good communicator and how to develop a good persuasive argument. He concluded that in order for a person to be a good influencer he had to have three things. If any one of these three components was missing, it would hinder the ability to influence others. Aristotle recognized that in order to be influential, we must have ethos, pathos, and logos.

Ethos is the ethical foundation of an argument. We must be ethical because our argument will be judged based on whether we are perceived as being ethical people or not. If we are not ethical then by association, our argument would not be ethical.

It is important to be ethical for another reason. As we seek to persuade people, we are taking away their free will or changing their way of thinking to our way of thinking through the use of influence. Because of this, we must be very careful about how we use the power of influence on our audience. If we are going to take something away from someone, it puts a responsibility upon us as speakers to have the greater interest of the audience in mind as we seek to influence them.

The second thing Aristotle said we need to have is pathos or passion. To be influential, we must be passionate about what we are trying to do. If we are not passionately invested in what we are trying to sell, how then can we expect the audience to be interested? It is not enough to just give the audience the information and let them determine how important it is. They are looking to the speaker to make a determination about how they should feel about the information. If we are passionate about our message then they will see this and be influenced by that message.

Lastly, we must be logical. This is usually not a problem today as people work very hard to put a lot of emphasis on the logos or logic of an argument. This is where speakers spend a majority of their time in the developmental phase of a presentation. If the argument is not logical, the speaker will lose credibility and may be thought of as a fool regardless of his passion or ethics. So as we are preparing our presentation we must remember the timeless principles Aristotle proposed so many years ago. To be influential we must ensure that we implement the three components of communications. Ethos, pathos and logos are essential to any persuasive presentation.

70

DO NOT ASK THE AUDIENCE TO PAY ATTENTION; CAPTURE THEIR ATTENTION.

As speakers, we strive to get the audience to pay attention to what we have to present. As we are putting together our presentation, we work diligently to include information that is relevant, important and applicable to the audience. As we are presenting the information, we are watching the audience and looking for indicators that they are paying attention to what we are presenting. When they are not looking at us, we conclude that they are not interested in what we spent so much time putting together just for them. What many speakers forget is that audiences listen with their ears and watch with their eyes. They may assume that when the audience is not looking at them, they are not listening either. This may not be the case. It is possible to not look at the speaker and still be listening but it is virtually impossible to be looking at the speaker and not be listening.

An audience may not be looking at the speaker because he is not doing anything. Watching some speakers is about as exciting as watching paint dry and we expect the audience to keep their eyes on him for the duration of a presentation. It is not fair to expect an audience to watch a speaker who is not doing anything. As speakers we do want the audience to be looking at us. Because we know it is difficult to watch someone and not listen, we want the audience to be looking at us. We also know that people learn more from their visual sense than any other sense so we are going to make sure that our body and hand gestures back up and reinforce what we are saying. In this way, we maximize the transfer potential of the information we are presenting.

As we are preparing our presentation, we must think about what kind of things command the attention of the audience. Movement is a good start. Movement attracts the attention of the audience so we want to move about as we are speaking and we want to use big hand gestures. Combining movement, hand gestures, good eye contact and command of our voice will help us to get the attention we desire. If we want the audience to look at us, we must give them something to look at. You cannot ask the audience to pay attention unless you capture their attention.

71

I AM IN CONTROL.

In order to implement all of the tools that a speaker has at his disposal, he must first come to terms with the fact that he is in control. There is a great deal of power associated with being a speaker and as with all power, it comes with a great responsibility. As we are working to influence an audience we must understand that we are not only in control of what we are doing but we are in control of the audience as well. We are stirring passions and emotions, thoughts and feelings as we speak. These are the characteristics of action and as we are arousing all of this in others, we are moving people toward action. Speakers have a heavy burden of responsibility as they communicate with an audience because they will always get the credit or the blame for the results of the presentation.

Two things that speakers must come to terms with are: there is no such thing as a boring topic, only boring speakers, and there is no such thing as a listless audience, only listless speakers. Speakers must grasp that there is no responsibility placed upon the audience to perform. That responsibility is the speaker's and his alone and he will own the outcome of his performance. I do not say this to make speakers nervous or put added pressure on them. These are just facts of nature that exist whether we accept them or not. If we do not understand this principle we might attempt to do things that will impact our presentation negatively.

Many speakers try to be low key and nearly invisible to the audience, thinking that this will lessen their responsibility. This is by no means the case. Hiding only makes it more apparent that the speaker is not comfortable and doesn't have a good grasp of his responsibilities. The sooner we are able to understand this, the better prepared we will be to understand how important it is to use and apply all of the tools that we have available to us as speakers. Our power comes from commanding the audience's attention and then using that attention to influence them. If we cannot take control, we as leaders, teachers or sales representatives will never be able to influence others. Since the results or outcome of our presentation are dependent entirely upon us, wouldn't it be in our interest to just stand up and take control of it from the start? Since it is our responsibility, let's own it and be in control. Ultimately the audience wants us to take charge. Audiences are more comfortable when they are led by someone who is confident and in control; when you are speaking, that is your responsibility. So in order to take advantage of all of the tools of influence available, you must first realize that you are in control.

72

START SLOWLY.

As speakers, we set the tone and pace for the audience. When we are nervous, the first thing that happens is our rate of speech increases. This can cause our words to come out faster than our brain can keep up. When this happens, we run into dead ends while our brain tries to catch up, causing long unwieldy pauses that can be difficult to recover from. Another reason that we tend to speak quickly is that when we experience anxiety, we want to get it over with as quickly as possible. The best way to get a speech over with is to speak as quickly as possible. If we start out at a high rate of speed, it is very difficult to slow down as we will feel the anxiety building in our system telling us to speed up.

By contrast, if we start our presentation speaking slowly, we draw our audience in by commanding the room with our presence and our self-confidence. We show the audience that we are in control and very comfortable with where we are and what we are doing. This is like being the captain of a ship and telling the crew to sit back and relax because I am in control and you have nothing to worry about. We want to reassure the audience that they will get exactly what they need and they will not have to worry about our skills as a communicator. Starting slowly tells the audience that we are in control of both ourselves and the audience.

Vocal variation is one of the most under-utilized aspects of our communication variables. Learning to take control of your pitch, power and pace can add incredible dimension to your presentation. Pitch, power and pace can bring your presentation to life. This is what makes storytellers so powerful. They have learned to use the power of their voice to project their feelings and emotions, transforming words into pictures. As speakers, we want to create word pictures or mental images for our audience to remember. We want to stir the emotions of the audience and stimulate them to remember what we are presenting. The next time you are getting ready to start your presentation, force yourself to start slowly. As you do this, you will feel yourself relax and gain confidence as you move into your presentation.

73

"THE PLAN IS NOTHING, BUT PLANNING IS EVERYTHING."

Dwight D Eisenhower said this as he was preparing for the D-Day invasion. It may seem as if Eisenhower was encouraging people not to have a plan but this was not the case. Planning is an integral part of any process no matter how simple or complex. The point that Eisenhower was making is that plans can change and often do. This does not mean that the process of developing the plan was not worthwhile. The very process that we go through in the development of the plan gives us that flexibility that we will need when things do not go as planned.

Planning gives us insight and understanding into the problems we are facing and helps us to recognize the strengths and weakness not only of our plan but of our capabilities as well. Planning forces us to take stock of the resources that we have available for the task at hand and then it helps us to determine how we can best apply these tools to accomplish our goal. This understanding helps to prepare us for the changes that will need to be made when we confront obstacles on our way to our goal. This evaluation of effort needed versus risk encountered helps us to determine if we are willing to do the task or not to do the task based on the risks involved versus the gain to be achieved with the accomplishment of the goal.

Risk comes in many forms. First, there is the physical risk we are all very familiar with. This is the risk of injury or death if things do not go right or the goal is not accomplished. Next, there is psychological risk associated with a task. As humans, we spend a great deal of time and energy protecting our image of ourselves. How we will look to others and how we will feel about ourselves if we fail becomes very important in our decision-making process. The psychological factors associated with risk quite often become the most important and powerful determiners of our actions. They are more powerful than all the other variables involved in the planning process. Our thoughts determine our attitude so our success or failure depends largely upon how we perceive the psychological risk associated with the task. Then, there is resource risk. We need to make an evaluation of the resources that will be expended in our effort to achieve our goal. This includes not only money and material but time and energy as well.

All of these risks must be evaluated with every task we are planning to undertake to ensure that the risk is worth the gain. This evaluation is part of the planning process and it prepares us for the task at hand. If we have objectively researched and thought through all of the contingencies as we work toward our goal, we have mentally prepared ourselves for the work, sacrifice and hardships that we may encounter along the way.

As you are preparing for any task, whether it is putting together a presentation or planning your career, take the time to think the whole process through and do as much planning as possible. No detail is too small that it should not be taken into consideration. "The plan is nothing, but planning is everything." It is the difference between success and failure in everything we do in life.

74

WE MUST LEARN TO BE WHERE THE PUCK IS GOING, NOT WHERE THE PUCK IS.

The great Canadian hockey player, Wayne Gretzky, has pointed out that lessons learned on the ice can have applications in life that are far-reaching. When you are chasing the puck, you are always behind it and catching it is determined by your speed (which is predictable) and the speed of the puck (which is much less predictable). Since you only control one of those two factors required to be successful in moving the puck into the opponent's net to score a goal, your success becomes more a matter of luck or chance rather than one of calculation and planning.

Many people choose to wait until they achieve a certain objective before they start behaving in a certain way. For example, I hear people say things like: I will start dressing better when I have a job that requires it, or I will start saving money when I have more money, or I will start taking better care of my house and car when I have a nicer one that I care more about. They are living in the moment and they are developing habits they will take with them into their future wherever they go. What they fail to recognize is that their future is being selected, based on their dress, attitude and performance right now. We do not make assessments of people based on where they want to be some day; we make our assessments of people based upon their actions, attitude, dress, and performance in the moment. Based on our evaluations, if people are dressing, acting and performing for where they are at a given moment, then that is where they belong. On the other hand, assessing potential is based on seeing people dress, act, and perform for something greater than where they are in the moment. We should determine where we want to be and what traits and qualities we would need to function there. Then we need to figure out how to incorporate these qualities into our present lives and develop habits that portray us as the person we desire to be.

We need to develop the skill of observing those in positions that we aspire to and then learn to emulate their habits. Many people believe they do not have enough time to do all this. What I have learned over the years is that we have time enough for everything that we find important. We make time for the things that are important to us. Rather than only living in the moment, we must learn to live, act, dress, perform and behave for a time and place where we aspire to be. Our situation will be determined by our attitude and behavior. What does your attitude and behavior say about you? Learn to be where the puck is going, not where the puck is.

75

YOU MISS EVERY SHOT YOU DON'T TAKE.

Life is a grand adventure, full of success and failures every day. We must come to terms with this and incorporate it into our daily lives. Some choose not to do anything. After all, if we never try, we can never fail and for many, the idea of failing at anything is one of their biggest fears. Life, however, is all about trying. It is about experiencing and taking charge. If we never try, we never succeed either

Winning is not everything but trying is everything. If we are unwilling to try, who knows what will be lost by our unwillingness to make the effort. What if the Wright brothers had never tried to fly; what if Louis Pasteur had never tried to find out what caused diseases; and what if Edison had not tried to develop the light bulb? They took a risk but they tried; because they tried, they worked through their many failures and did great things for the world. For each of these individuals, their successes were a snapshot from their lives, a defining moment that led to each of them becoming household names.

This snapshot, however is not the movie of their entire lives. Each of these men endured many setbacks and failures throughout their lifetimes. They did not just wake up one morning and build a plane or invent a light bulb or discover bacteria. The movie of their lives is an extended story about trying things that had not been done or that were thought to be impossible. By their willingness to try, they succeeded in doing something that had never been done before. They missed thousands and thousands of shots before they finally made one that scored and that was the score heard around the world.

What is the movie of your life? Success in life is not about the singular defining achievement but it is a record of how we live. Life can be a grand adventure of discovery or it can be a terrifying nightmare of discontent. Nothing is certain in life and no one can guarantee us success but I can certainly guarantee a formula for failure. All you have to do to fail is to do nothing and the results will be entirely unimpressive. We miss every shot we don't take in life so don't be afraid to take as many shots as your life allows you.

76

COURAGE IS NOT THE ABSENCE OF FEAR; IT IS THE ABILITY TO DO WHAT IS RIGHT IN THE FACE OF IT.

Courage is a very interesting characteristic. It is often misidentified or misused in describing a person or an act that is observed by others. Courage is the ability to face our fears and do what is right even as we confront those fears. Every day we observe acts that many people mislabel as courage; for example, skydivers jumping out of airplanes or firemen going into burning buildings or perhaps mountain climbers hanging on a cliff. Each of these tasks is inherently dangerous and the first few times someone attempted them, he would experience all of the physiological effects associated with being scared. His heart rate would increase, his eyes would dilate, his blood pressure would rise, he would begin to sweat, his ability to perform fine motor functions would decrease, cognitive ability would begin to shut down, the instinctive response mechanism of fight or flight would kick in, his hands would begin to shake due to the increase of adrenalin. All of these conditions occur in response to a perceived threat. It is a body's way of preparing itself for attack and possible trauma.

One might ask then, why all these efforts occur even when we are not afraid of something happening to us physically. After all, I don't think a rational person believes that being physically assaulted or hurt is similar to standing up and delivering a speech. But even irrational fear or anxiety triggers an autonomic response to threat whether it is perceived as physical or as psychological. These feelings and responses are designed to protect us as well as to guide our actions. The key to courage is being able to focus on what is right and to perform appropriately in that moment when our mind is trying to tell us not to be there at all.

Courage is not the absence of fear but the ability to do what is right in the face of fear. Many of the acts mentioned above are courageous acts but over time, with exposure and training, they become commonplace to the people who perform them. For many people who place themselves in potentially dangerous situations, it is the thrill and excitement of the situation that they enjoy. Through stress inoculation they have become comfortable being uncomfortable and have even learned to enjoy the experience of being excited by the element of danger associated with the task.

Courage got them through it the first couple of times but eventually they reached a point where they were driven by the rush of the excitement. They are channeling into their performance the energy they receive from it.

This is where we want to be in our own performance, no longer being controlled by our fear. People perceived as courageous have learned to be in control and to rely on their knowledge to empower them. We want to reach a point where we are empowered in the face of our fears. The best way to do this is to face those fears and train ourselves to become comfortable in environments that we find stressful or uncomfortable. The next time you find yourself afraid to do something, remember that courage is not the absence of fear but the ability to do what is right in the face of that fear.

77

WE ALL SUFFER FROM SELF-DOUBT.

There is a prevailing impression that people who are confident and appear unafraid as they stand up before audiences have no self-doubts. Anyone who has ever stood before an audience has asked himself, "what am I doing here?" In much the same way, an audience asks itself as they observe a speaker, "why is what this person saying important to me and why am I allowing this to influence me today?" There are a couple of things we can do that will help us to get past the periods of self-doubt.

First, we need to have a good grasp of what our purpose is in life. As long as our purpose is bigger than ourselves, we generally will come up with the right answer. If it all comes down to personal gain, we can fall very flat. It has been said that a person all wrapped up in himself makes a very small package. This is especially true when that person is trying to influence others. As we stand before an audience, we need to have a purpose bigger than ourselves. When self-doubt starts to creep into our thoughts, we simply have to remind ourselves of our ultimate purpose. If we are just in it for ourselves then we will have a hard time overcoming our self-doubt. If, however, we are doing it for the benefit of others, to help them grow and learn and develop, then we will easily overcome our doubts. It is easy to be confident when what we are doing is for the benefit of others.

Another thing that we can do is to develop a good support structure to help keep us on track. This includes having a close group of trusted friends and mentors who will tell us the truth. As our mind begins to wander into the zone of self-doubt, these supportive people can help us to keep a positive perspective.

Lastly, I recommend that you take every opportunity presented to you to train. There is nothing like training to help you gain a good understanding of how to improve your performance and develop your self-confidence. The next time you start to question yourself, make sure you have developed the defenses necessary to protect yourself from self-doubt. It is not a bad thing to question yourself, but make sure you find the right answer. We all suffer from self-doubt at one time or another but we must remember our higher purpose and move on to self-confidence.

78

FAILURE IS SIMPLY THE LEARNING PROCESS OF SUCCESS.

What is your perspective? What happens to you psychologically and physiologically when you encounter failure? How do you process the information when things do not work out the way that you wanted or expected them to? The bottom line in life is that things are not always going to work the way you want or expect and when they don't, you have a choice of how you are going to process that failure.

In our quest for perfection we have developed what we call a zero tolerance society, a society where we expect success the first time every time in ourselves and others. Our quest for perfection can be a blessing or a curse depending on how we deal with it. Striving for perfection is a good thing unless the fear of failure keeps us from even trying. Many people internalize their work, believing it to be a personal reflection on themselves. Thus, if the work fails, they feel as though they have failed as a person.

Failure is a learning process in life and the sooner we recognize this, the sooner we will be able to use it as a tool to enhance our lives. Our failures provide us with tremendous learning opportunities not only about the task at hand but about ourselves as well. The attitude that we take into our failures will determine how much we learn from them. Many people want to run away from their failures as fast as they can. It is far better to take some time to analyze the failure and use it as an opportunity.

Performance is a product of two things, execution and environment. Both are essential to a successful performance. Flawless execution within the wrong environment can produce poor results. Execution is something over which, with training, we can attain nearly perfect control. Environment, on the other hand, is constantly evolving and changing and it has far more variables than can ever be fully accounted for. You can have flawless execution but every once in a while, you get a curve ball in your environment that results in your performance being something less than perfection.

Life is a continual learning process. How we interpret feedback will determine how effective we are at making changes that will produce positive results in our lives. Feedback is neither good nor bad, it just is. If we interpret the feedback as negative then we run the risk of learning nothing from it and in our fear of it, we may avoid or ignore what could be gained. On the other hand, if we interpret all feedback as good, we have an opportunity to learn from it and apply the lessons learned, incorporating them into our execution so that next time we can improve. Failure is just the learning process of success.

#79

THREE PARTS OF A SPEECH

Any time you must put a presentation together, it is valuable to know the three parts of a speech. This knowledge will help you balance your presentation so that you give the appropriate amount of time and energy to those parts of the presentation that will provide you with the greatest return. Content, organization and delivery all must be managed to ensure the success of an influential endeavor.

Content is the first part of a speech that must be considered. This is the knowledge development phase of your presentation. It is tough to give a presentation if you do not know what you are talking about. It is important to do the research in order to gain a thorough understanding of the topic that you are going to present. An often overlooked part of this research that should be included is researching the background of your audience and determining why this subject is important to them. As you might imagine, content is the part of speech preparation where speakers spend most of their time.

The next part of a speech is organization. Great information based on thorough research that is not properly organized can confuse the audience more than it helps. Many speakers conduct their research and then organize the information properly only to get nervous during their presentation and neglect to make use of their notes. They start to ramble citing random facts that take them on tangents and make it difficult for them to stay on point. Another common mistake is for the speaker to break his presentation down into bullet points and then fail to highlight the points for the audience. When the speaker is done, the audience may have ten points but not know which ones were key. If a speaker announces, for example, that he is going to provide four reasons why you should buy his product today, then he must highlight those four reasons sufficiently enough for the audience to remember and act on them. If they cannot do this, then the speaker was not effective and had not organized his presentation properly.

The final part of a speech is delivery. This is often the part of the presentation that gets the least amount of time spent on it and yet it is the most important when it comes to the overall effectiveness of the presentation. While many speakers will dedicate a great deal of time to the memorization of their presentation, they will generally give much less consideration to their pitch, power and pace. Many speakers have grand ideas in the planning stage of their presentation and think that they are going to do all sorts of things while they are on stage. Once the presenter gets there, however, the habitual process takes over and many of those great ideas are not manifested in the presentation. The best way to ensure that our ideas will come to fruition once we are on stage is to practice all of the actions necessary to project in the most realistic environment possible. In order for our presentation to be effective and influential, we must ensure that we give the proper time and consideration to all three parts of a speech.

80

BETTER A GRAND FAILURE THAN A MEDIOCRE SUCCESS.

Jack Welch, former C.E.O. of General Electric, told this to his senior executives. He had little tolerance for any lack of progress. He wanted to see people put it all on the line and fearlessly give it their best. Unfortunately, fear controls us much more than we might think. Physical fear dictates many of our actions but psychological fear does so to an even greater extent. We spend a great deal of energy in life trying to find a place to be comfortable, a place where we are safe from the physical and psychological effects of fear. Finding a comfort zone can be very difficult and once we find it, we tend to build very high, thick, heavy, strong walls around it to protect us from everything. We lock ourselves into this safe area by establishing habits that ensure that we do not stray outside of the boundaries of this protective wall.

It is good to have a safe place in our lives that we can go to but it is not good to live there. Life is an adventure that is meant to be lived and playing it safe all the time will limit our potential. This is not to say that we should disregard those things that are in place to ensure our personal safety. This is more about taking psychological risk. Failure, like success, is a part of growing. Too many people are so afraid of failure that they never try anything new or take a chance; therefore their potential to grow is never recognized. A friend of mine once told me, "Until I try to do that which I have not already mastered, I will not grow." He said he was very comfortable doing what he did and he was very good at it, but only to a certain level of performance. He could have continued performing at this level for much longer but to do so would have kept him from recognizing and realizing his full potential.

My friend told me, "I had to get comfortable being uncomfortable and get out of my safe zone in order to grow. When I did, I certainly was not perfect, nor was I comfortable, but my growth was tremendous. I recognized that I could do things that I never thought imaginable because I was willing to try."

You never know what you can do until you try. This is one of the things that has made the U.S. Navy SEAL teams so successful. When I was a young lad just starting out in the SEAL teams, I heard a saying that was a mantra for all SEALs: Go big or go home. SEALs were not tolerant of people who showed up and weren't willing to put it all on the line. Regardless of the difficulties or complexities involved, everyone had to try. In trying, SEALs learn a lot about themselves.

Inside of each and every one of us is a potential that is unlimited, we have to be willing to try to recognize that potential and to act on it. This means taking risks and making changes and knowing that we will not always succeed, but having the courage to try regardless of the size or complexity of the task involved. It means getting out of our comfort zone and experiencing all that life has to offer. At the end of the day, it is better a grand failure than a mediocre success.

81

THE COMPANY WE KEEP BECOMES A REFLECTION OF OURSELVES.

All of us are much more a product of our environment than we might think. The choice of friends and associates is a factor that impacts us in many ways that need to be considered as we are making decisions about our life pursuits and our goals. Many of these influences of those around us are more subtle than they might first appear, but the impact they have on our perception may be very powerful. Although many of the different environments in our world may seem to intertwine, they often establish defining points for specific groups of people. For example, a restaurant that is appropriate for family dining at 7:00 in the evening may not be so appropriate for family dining at 1:00 in the morning when the wet tee-shirt competition starts. Many organizations vary their offerings to appeal to a broader spectrum of clientele to ensure that they get their share of the available market.

A person's behavior is not always reflective of his intentions. He may well stand in church on Sunday morning only to find himself picking fights at the local bar the following Friday night after a few too many. As we may be interpreted by others based on our environment, we are equally judged by the company with whom we associate. Choosing the right friends cannot be overstated. It is vital to socialize and interact with people who do the right things for the right reasons, not those who make poor choices and decisions. We are judged by our choices in our daily endeavors just as we judge others in the same fashion. Environment has a lot to do with how we perceive situations and events and it has a lot of impact on how others perceive us.

This is not to say that we have to act as though we are better than others or that we should shun people who are not like us but it does provide signals. Good habits are the product of hard work and discipline and they take years to build. Good habits are fragile, however, and they can be easily destroyed by bad influences. Many a good person has been brought down by people he thought he was helping.

As we aspire to learn and grow, we should surround ourselves with people who act, dress, talk, and perform according to the place where we want to be. This encourages us and provides a guide for us to follow as we pursue our goals. On the other hand, if we surround ourselves with people who do not share our aspirations and goals, they may hold us back or even pull us down by making us question our own behavior. Also, as others assess our friends, they are also forming opinions about us. If our friends are perceived as not being of like mind and good character, it is quite likely that we will be found wanting as well.

This is not about being snooty or uppity but it is a fact of life that we must recognize as we identify our goals and determine where we want to be in our lives. There is nothing like having people of like mind to help hold us accountable for our actions in life. Knowing that others we respect may be disappointed if we make the wrong decision, we are influenced in ways that we cannot even imagine. Take stock of your life and look around at the people you call friends. Are they people who hold you accountable to do the right things or are they people who are just as likely to encourage you to do the wrong thing, perhaps so that they will not have to examine their own actions in life? Ultimately, we must remember that the company we keep is a reflection of ourselves.

82

SUCCESSFUL PEOPLE ARE NOT LUCKY; THEY ARE DOING SOMETHING RIGHT AND DOING IT CONSISTENTLY.

Have you ever looked at someone and based upon the success you observe in their life said to yourself, "man, they're lucky?" For many people, this is a way of avoiding the hard work and discipline that is required to be successful; for others, it is actually a belief that they hold. It is easy to look at someone and put all of the reasons for their success into a category called luck, but luck is not generally the pivotal cause of success or failure.

People generally make their own luck through good planning and preparing and then by doggedly seeking out the opportunity that will lead to success. Luck, as most of us define it, really has very little to do with success but it is much easier for us to justify the success of others by labeling the cause of their success as luck. Most of us recognize that this is not the case, however. Lucky people have developed good habits through discipline and hard work and have kept their eyes open for an opportunity to capitalize upon their hard work.

Many opportunities randomly come into our lives every day. Some of these opportunities are good and some of them are not so good depending upon what we aspire to be or do in our lives. The key is to know how the choices we make will affect our ultimate goal. You may have an opportunity to take a nap or finish that homework that you need to get done for school tomorrow. You may have an opportunity to watch a television program or fix the leaking faucet in the bathroom. You may have an opportunity to take a trip or go to college for a semester. Each of these offers a choice and the choice you make will add to or detract from your opportunities.

Each of the above examples seems to represent an easy choice of what is good or what is bad. Life, however, is not so simple. Each of the above alternatives might have a place in time where it represents a good choice. For example, taking a nap or doing homework? Doing that homework may seem the obvious right choice but if you are tired and the quality of your work will suffer because of it, then perhaps you need a nap before you do your homework. You must make good choices in the little things to ensure that the bigger opportunities will come.

As we identify a personal goal, we must plan for reaching that goal and then prepare ourselves for what it will take to move us toward the goal when we find the opportunity. The next time you see someone who is successful, take a step back and look carefully at what that person did that prepared him for being successful and then figure out how to incorporate those habits into your life. We can learn a lot from people who are successful but we must realize that they are not just lucky. Successful people are doing something right and doing it consistently.

83

IF SUCCESS WAS EASY, EVERYONE WOULD HAVE IT.

We are all a living in the "now" generation where everything is fast. We want what we want and we want it immediately if not sooner. Our demand for high-speed responses to our desires has affected us physically and mentally. Physically, we have become so used to massive amounts of stimuli that we have difficulty focusing on specific things because there is so much going on. We are breeding Attention Deficit Disorder into our lives through massive quantities of stimuli. Mentally, we also are accustomed to high-speed responses to our needs and when that does not happen we become very frustrated. We are losing the ability to use critical analysis as we assess things in our lives. There is too much information for us to process in the time available so we simply look for the apparent major point of any event and move on. This can have the effect of giving us a very skewed perspective of events.

As we observe an event, we simplify the process into what we perceive as its most basic apparent form without taking into consideration the thousands of tiny details associated with the event. For example, when we look at someone who is successful, we tend to see only the success. When we attempt to duplicate what we see in that moment, we do not understand why it does not work the same way for us. The great boxer Muhammad Ali once said that he was not made a champion in the ring, he was simply recognized there. He had put in a lot of work that was not visible to the public to become the champion that he was. What many people fail to realize is that there were years spent developing knowledge, skills, habits and abilities that have come together at this point in time enabling this person to achieve the results witnessed at that moment and interpreted as success. This can be very frustrating to a society that is used to the quick fix and rapid response to their every desire.

We must come to realize that there is a process of development that is associated with every task and it is very seldom that this process can be cut short regardless of our desires or abilities. You may have a tremendous knowledge of the human body and have a desire to be a medical doctor, but you will not be a medical doctor without going through the years of education required to become a doctor. There are certain processes in life designed to ensure that people who are not capable of performing at a certain level are not allowed to advance to the highest levels of performance. We must have a thorough understanding of the processes associated with the goals that we set for ourselves in life. The better we understand these processes, the better prepared we will be to work toward and to achieve our goals and the less likely we will be disappointed when we come upon requirements associated with the task. The next time you observe someone who is successful, remember that you are only witnessing the moment. You are not seeing the years of hard work and sacrifice that went into achieving that success and arriving at that moment in time. If it was easy, everyone would do it.

84

GOOD IS THE ENEMY OF GREAT.

Attitude plays a huge role in our successes and failures in life. For many of us, the term 'good' is a goal we set for ourselves in many of the various tasks that we perform in our daily life. The problem with 'good' is that it is such an ambiguous term. 'Good' is only relative to the people we are being compared with and the audience that the evaluation is coming from. When my daughter was in grade school she was a good runner. She was good relative to her other classmates of the same age based on the interpretation of the teachers at that school. However, this really does not say very much about my daughter's running ability. As seekers of success, we need to refine our definitions in order to enhance our interpretation of our performance.

'Good' has become a catchword today for any performance that meets the average requirements of the task. If someone says you are 'doing good' they really mean you are perfectly average. It is hard to get accurate feedback from people in today's society because in our effort to not hurt people's feelings or damage their self-worth, we lump just trying into the category of 'good'. Feedback is the key to improving performance, but without accurate feedback that is specific to the needed changes in execution to modify performance, then it is basically worthless.

Excellence should be our goal as we work to develop our skills at any task. A key element to remember here is that every task is made up of many subtasks or small tasks that come together to contribute to the ultimate outcome of the process. For example, in golf, how we hold the club has a substantial impact on performance. In public speaking, how we move or look people in the eye or use our voice will have a major impact on how the audience interprets what we are saying. Each of these elements individually may not seem to be very important but when they are all taken together and they are done correctly, they have a synergy that makes them very effective. We must identify all of the skills associated with our task and ensure that we understand their impact on the ultimate performance we seek to achieve.

Being satisfied with 'good' is to be satisfied with being average. If we truly want to be successful, we must become dissatisfied and intolerant with 'good' and become seekers of excellence in everything we do. When we do this, we will start to see growth that we never thought imaginable. We are meant for greatness in our lives. God did not put us on this earth to be average; He put us on earth to glorify His name and this is not done by being satisfied with average. Each of us has a destiny to fulfill and it can only be found when we recognize that 'good' is the enemy of Great.

85

GREAT LEADERS TAKE MORE RESPONSIBILITY THAN THEY SHOULD WHEN THINGS GO WRONG AND LESS CREDIT THAN THEY SHOULD WHEN THINGS GO RIGHT.

Few topics in business have been the subject of so much scrutiny as leadership. Leadership may very well be the simplest and most complicated aspect of a business. There are many theories on leadership and for the student of leadership these can present a difficult field to maneuver. Most of the models that have been developed over the years address one aspect or another of the leadership concept but most have difficulty simplifying the process to a system that is easy to follow. Some systems require the study of psychology to understand the different personalities of leaders and followers. Other methodologies require the study of historic leaders and the student risks becoming schizophrenic in an attempt to adapt his personality style to the style of various leaders encountered in the study. Both of these methods often require that the student of them spend more time researching and studying other people than doing his own job.

As leaders, we have responsibilities and although it is important to know and understand the people you respect and admire, it is also important that we do our job as well. Leadership is about people and a leader who cares about others will let them know how important they are. People recognize when they are respected by their leaders and they will respond in kind. On the other hand, when they do not feel respected they may respond with actions that are contrary to what most leaders are seeking.

One of the best ways that a leader can show respect for others is to give them credit for the work they do. Leaders are often perceived as the person responsible for the accomplishment of a particular task but in reality, a leader is nothing without his team. There is a voice inside each of us that tells us we need to get the credit for a successful outcome so that we can be recognized and rewarded for our efforts. This voice is our ego and it will harm our credibility as a leader. As leaders, we need to ensure that the team gets the credit for jobs that go well and it is our job to make sure the team is recognized. Conversely, when things do not go smoothly, then it is the responsibility of the leader to step up for his people. This means that leaders have to be willing to take the heat when things do not go well. It can be hard as a leader to bear the brunt of the responsibility but that risk is part of the job. Remember to show your respect for your people by giving them the credit when things go right and taking more responsibility than you deserve when things go wrong.

86

NO ONE CARES HOW MUCH I KNOW UNTIL THEY KNOW HOW MUCH I CARE.

Knowledge is definitely a trait that people look for in their leaders but is a trait that sometimes can be overrated by the leader himself. It is important to make the right decisions in the course of business, but making the right decision is secondary to taking care of your people. Because people are the key to the success of any business, leaders must never lose sight of the fact that they are the reason that their business continues to exist. Without our people, there is no process to guide, no business to develop. Business is built in response to the demand for a product and our people fulfill that demand.

It is no easy process to identify a market and build a product that can be sold in that market. The truth is that only about one in 30 concepts make it out of the good idea department and only one in 20 of these become a product that can sustain a business. With those kinds of odds, a business person definitely has to be smart in order to bring an idea to fruition. It takes a tremendous amount of knowledge and almost unlimited energy to turn a good idea into a marketable product and there are many pitfalls along the way. From idea to design, to prototype, to production, to marketing, to sustainment of roles, there are thousands of turns, many of which will lead to dead ends. There have been many great ideas that never resulted in a product because there just was not a demand for that product. In the process of developing a business, intelligence will help a leader to navigate the tricky road between idea and profit.

As complicated, difficult and important as all of this is, however, it pales in comparison to the importance of people. No great idea can be brought to fruition without the support of people who are willing to dedicate their time and energy to its development. These people become the cornerstone of any great project and without them the vision is doomed. While it is important to be smart when dealing with business matters, it is also important to be smart when caring about your people. One of the best ways to demonstrate this is to show respect.

Showing respect for people whether they work for us or are part of an audience that we want to influence goes a long way toward developing a positive relationship of understanding and caring. As long as people feel as though they matter, they will work diligently for an organization that cares about them. On the other hand, when people do not feel as though they matter, they will go to great lengths to develop systems of self-preservation to ensure that their interests are cared for. As you navigate the minefield of business, remember that it is not all about the process. People provide the energy that drives the process and without them the process goes nowhere. No one cares how much I know until they know how much I care.

87

THE BEST WAY TO PREDICT THE FUTURE IS TO CREATE IT.

How nice it would be to have a crystal ball that we could use to predict the future. It is human nature to want to know what is going to happen before it happens. Armed with this type of knowledge we could make choices that would give us our greatest return. If we could read the future, we could invest our time, energy, resources and money in a way that would ensure that we achieved the greatest benefits and failure would be virtually impossible. If only we had the crystal ball, we would all succeed at everything we attempted because we would know what the outcome of our actions would be and if we did not like the results, we would simply change our actions until we obtained the results we were seeking.

Unfortunately, we do not have crystal balls to tell us the future. In place of our crystal ball, we must analyze data to develop projected models based on past performance to determine probable future results. In determining our future, this is an iffy methodology at best. The human factor makes the variables far too unpredictable to develop results that are reliable or consistent. People have a complex assortment of wishes, wants, dreams and desires that are almost impossible to predict. Although science has made it possible to make some basic predictions about human behavior, based on years of collected research data, it is impossible to say for certain what people will do or how they will react in various scenarios.

People are amazing! Every person is a wealth of limitless potential that is as unpredictable as the stock market. Their individual actions are the greatest determiner of their future and although some predictions can be made based on their current circumstances, there will always be someone who blows the bell curve away because they possess the will, the strength of character and the determination to do or be something different than would be suggested by their situation or their status. These are the people who defy the odds by standing up and saying, "I will not be a statistic."

Life can have a dumbing-down effect that may lead us to believe that where we are is where we belong. Following the actions of the herd is safe in that it ensures that you will be exactly like the rest of the herd but it seldom produces spectacular results. For those who try to be different and challenge the herd, the future will be determined by who they are on the inside rather than the actions of other people and the events that are happening around them. It takes a strong person to challenge his or her circumstances and dare to be different. When they do, they have taken the first step toward creating their own future. The future is only unpredictable for those who are unwilling to dream of something better and it takes personal action to make it happen. The best way to predict the future is to create it.

88

P = P–I

I have always liked the idea of breaking complex processes down to their most basic components. Life itself can be so complex that sometimes it is hard to see those things that form the foundation of our success or failure. It is like looking at a jigsaw puzzle. If you first put all of the like colors together in categories, it makes the rest of the process so much easier to traverse. We need to do the same thing with our goals in life. We need to identify the process that is going to help us achieve the goal and then identify the resources that we have available to work toward the goal; and lastly, we need to identify the obstacles that we know we will have to overcome along the way.

This is all part of the planning process. P=P-I is a great little formula that Scott Eblin talks about in his book, *The Next Level.* Performance equals Potential minus Interference. We all have an unlimited wealth of potential, both physically and mentally, but interferences sap our potential and keep it from being recognized. Interference can come in two forms. It can be physical or it can be mental. Physical interference includes such things as money, transportation, support, time, obligations, and many other elements that keep us from achieving our potential. The mental obstacles are much more detrimental, however. Mental interference comes in the form of self-doubt, fear, lack of confidence, poor self-image and self-loathing just to name a few.

Taking all of these elements of interference into account and subtracting them from our potential will enable us to determine our performance every time. The good news is that potential is a constant of "UNLIMITED." That means that the only thing we have to do is work diligently to eliminate the mental and physical interferences that we encounter along the way toward our goal. As we assess the amount and type of interference in our life, we need to take stock of the resources at our disposal as well: our good health, support structure, education, opportunity, etc. It should be noted that quite often the resources we have available to us can become interferences as well and we need to be willing to work around them or to remove them from our lives. One example of a resource that can become an interference is owning a house that is more than you can afford and choosing to keep it even though the payments on that house keep you from having the money to go back to school.

Taking stock of your interferences and the recourses available to alleviate them enables you to minimize the negative and accentuate the positive in your life. When you are working toward a goal, remember to subtract the interferences in your life as much as possible and never forget that you have unlimited potential. P=P-I

89

AUDIENCES ARE VERY SMART.

Although audiences can be very diverse in many areas, there are a few constants that a speaker wanting to influence an audience must keep in mind. Adult audiences regardless of formal education have a lifetime of experience. These experiences have given them a broad background of knowledge that could never be gained in a classroom. Whatever their level of education, audiences know what feels right and what feels wrong, often beginning with the moment a presenter steps onto a stage. Within a matter of just a few seconds they have applied their lifetime of experience and have developed an opinion using what Malcolm Gladwell refers to as rapid cognition in his book *Blink*. The impression that is formed in those first few critical seconds will carry into how the audience will interpret the rest of the presentation. If the audience feels that the presenter does not live up to their expectations, that presenter could easily lose credibility at the very beginning and never regain it. Consequently, the presenter will fail to have any positive influence on the audience.

Many of the elements that an audience will use to make a judgment or develop an impression about a speaker are things that we cannot change; for example, sex, race, height, circumstances and location of the meeting. On the other hand, there are elements that a presenter does have influence over but which can be very difficult to change. These include such things as accent, language use, weight, presentation style and forum setting. Then, there are some things that are easily changed such as posture, attire, grooming, facial gestures, vocal inflection, and makeup. All of these elements have a tremendous influence on how the audience will interpret a speaker and consequently how they will feel about him. If their rapid cognition tells them that this speaker doesn't seem to be the appropriate person to be delivering the message then it is likely that they will not be open to being influenced. On the other hand, if the presentation makes them feel good and is in alignment with what they expected, then it is quite likely they will be influenced.

How a presenter is perceived by an audience is based upon an infinite number of tiny variables. Some of these variables can be managed while others are beyond the speaker's control. Great communicators are recognized as people who possess the ability to influence audiences toward their ideas, visions or goals. If we want to be influential in our communications process, we must take control of as many of the communication variables as we possibly can to ensure that we project the image or message that we want to project. Communications is so much more than the words we say. It is every facet of our being that projects an image to the audience and they, in turn, will interpret every subtle nuance to the best of their ability based on their own life experiences. So take control of every aspect of your presentation and never forget that audiences are very smart.

90

A LEADER IS A PERSON
WITH A VISION
AND THE ABILITY TO
ARTICULATE THAT VISION
SO VIVIDLY AND SO
POWERFULLY THAT IT
BECOMES THE
VISION OF OTHERS.

Jack Welch was renowned for his leadership concepts and this principle says a lot about his expectation of a leader. Jack was a great communicator and he had an amazing ability to infuse an audience with a vision. It is important for a leader to have a vision but this is certainly not enough. Any person who professes to be a "self-made man" is a person who has not yet learned one of the essential keys to success. No one is self-made. Any person who has ever achieved any status will tell you that he was supported by many people in his life: family, mentors, motivators, teachers, trainers, colleagues, coaches, supporters, customers, employees, bosses, supervisors, friends and other persons or groups who helped him directly or indirectly. A boss is nothing without his employees, a salesman is nothing without his customers, a politician is nothing without his constituents, and a pro athlete is nothing without the coach, the team and the fans that support him. So how can anyone say that he is self-made?

Everyone needs support of some kind to see their dreams come to fruition. As we create networks to support us in life's endeavors, we must have a vision. That vision is just the first step. We must be able to get others interested in our vision. This is not easy. For others to become interested in supporting our vision, it must become their vision. We need to develop the ability to communicate our vision so well that other people can see it and visualize its importance to them. The words we choose and how we use these words will determine how others interpret the vision that we present and understand how that vision relates to them. This will be the determining factor of whether or not they will support that vision.

In order to convince people to support us in our quest, we must inspire, motivate and influence our audience and help them not only to understand and see our vision but to accept it as their own and to want it as badly as we do. We want our audience to internalize our vision and own it. Once we recognize the audience's potential we can work together toward a common goal.

One of author Steven J. Covey's *Seven Habits of Highly Successful People* is to seek first to understand and then endeavor to be understood. His point is that if you want to have success in working with another individual or a group, you must be able to understand their needs as well as they do. This can only be done if you are open-minded and willing to listen to what others are trying to express. In much the same way, we want our support network to understand and believe in our vision so well that they can articulate it as well or even better than we can. In this manner, we duplicate ourselves and spread our own vision to others. As you are working toward energizing your group toward a common goal, remember that it will be your ability to articulate your vision so vividly and so powerfully that it will influence them to accept it as their vision also. That will be the key to your success.

91

LEARN TO PUT YOUR HANDS AT YOUR SIDE.

Habitual conditioning is one of the most difficult things to change and not keeping our hands at our sides is no exception. For many speakers, comfort is all about putting barriers between themselves and their audience. A barrier is anything that separates a person emotionally and physically from an audience. For some speakers, the more barriers between themselves and the audience, the more emotionally protected they will feel.

Barriers come in many forms and the training, comfort and confidence of the speaker will determine how many he feels are necessary. Physical barriers include such things as podiums, chairs, tables, lecterns, books, or other items placed or held in front of the body, including hands, and the distance maintained between the speaker and the audience.

Emotional barriers are those that we project with our body language, crossing our arms, failure to make eye contact, not turning our bodies toward people when we talk to them, not showing emotion, lack of movement, standing in the fig leaf position and clasping the hands together in front of us. All of these gestures are designed to give comfort and stability to a speaker attempting to communicate with an audience.

What to do with those hands???? Developing a good selection of hand use is difficult and requires a lot of coaching and feedback. Many speakers clasp their hands in front of them and telegraph a lot of anxiety to their audience by wrenching on their fingers until the audience is sure that one of those fingers is going to break or by clenching their hands so tightly that they are white-knuckled even as they are attempting to appear comfortable and relaxed.

Great speakers must learn to put their hands at their sides avoiding the temptation of putting those hands in their pockets. Hands in pockets are an absolute no-no. If we put our hands in our pockets we will be tempted to play with the change or any keys we find there. Even if we don't succumb to this distraction we are still restricting our use of gestures by confining the hands to our pockets. By learning to place our hands comfortably at our side, we avoid using them as a barrier and we make them readily available for hand gestures as needed to produce maximum effect for our audience. Because most speakers have developed other habitual processes in the use of their hands, placing them at their sides will feel unnatural at first and it will require a lot of practice to learn to keep them there. Don't become your own worst enemy by putting barriers between you and your audience. Learn to put your hands down at your sides.

92

DISCONTENT IS THE FIRST STEP FORWARD IN THE PROGRESS OF A MAN.

Every great achievement of man through the centuries was the product of someone being dissatisfied. They were either dissatisfied with the work they were doing and wanted an easier way to do it or with just not knowing the answer to a question. Whatever the reason, they were dissatisfied with the way things were and they wanted to explore other alternatives. For some, the motivation to action was as simple as the one presented by Sir Edmund Hillary when he was asked why he wanted to climb Mount Everest. "Because it was there," he said. He was dissatisfied with not being able to do something and was going to do whatever it took to climb Everest.

As we maneuver our way through life, we must be careful to avoid being lulled into complacency. It is easy to find ourselves in a position where we become spectators watching life pass us by rather than participants living the grand adventure. Life is meant to be an adventure of discovery and that means that we are programmed to be a little dissatisfied with not knowing the answers to all our questions. With every discovery, we learn a little more not only about our world but also about ourselves. The thrill and rush of learning or doing something that we did not know or have not done can never be taken away from us regardless of how many others came before us. Every first step forward begins with a sense of dissatisfaction of where we are and a desire for something different.

There are many things in life that keep us from embarking on adventures and experiencing the joy of discovery including self-doubt, being lazy, being uninterested and the fear of what we might encounter. We all have an endless wealth of potential but we can never realize that potential if we do not become dissatisfied with where we are in life and begin to take chances. When we try, we learn so much about not only the endeavor that we have chosen to pursue but about ourselves. How we react to the feedback we receive to our effort and hard work says a lot about us.

The next time you find yourself feeling discontent with something, embrace that feeling and recognize it as an opportunity to expand yourself and to make changes for the better. As you do this, you will grow and learn even more about yourself and the world around you. Discontent is the first step on the path to the successful achievement of a goal.

93

CONSTANTLY CHALLENGE YOURSELF TO BE THE BEST EVERY DAY.

Life is a wonderful journey with highs and lows that we all must deal with. No matter who you are or what your position in life, there are going to be good days and there are going to be bad days. One of the amazing things about success is that once it has been achieved, other people seldom see all of the hard times that the successful person had to endure or overcome to get there. We have a tendency to only see the results rather than the hard work and struggles that were a part of the process of successfully achieving a goal. Success is a journey with lots of rocky places in the road between the start and the finish line. These rocky obstacles can take many forms from poverty or lack of support to mistakes and self-doubt. How we deal with these hard times shapes our destiny.

The hard times can be very public as was the case with Winston Churchill when he decided to invade the Dardanelles during World War I which resulted in a catastrophic defeat of the allied forces. Or it can be private as with Thomas Edison who was asked to leave grade school because he asked too many questions and he had to teach himself in the local public library. Whether public or private, the hard times are there for everyone and the character of each individual determines how he/she deals with them.

Anyone who has ever achieved any amount of success in his life will have a story of struggle to share. The observed results are generally what motivate us to want to emulate the successful person. It is easy to be motivated by these results, often readily apparent such as status, cars, homes, lifestyle, celebrity, or any of the other outward manifestations of success. The problem with this is that we seldom see the struggle and hard work that person had to endure and the setbacks he had to overcome.

One of the key principles that every successful person has mastered is the ability to renew himself every day. Recognizing that there will be struggles and setbacks ahead can help to prepare us for what we will face. Every day, we have to start fresh and we must challenge ourselves yet again. Regardless of what happened yesterday, today is a new day and we must approach it as though it is the first day of the rest of our lives. Every day is a new day and we must not waste it sulking about losses or celebrating the victories of the day before. Today is a gift to be cherished and used to its fullest potential.

Everything in life exists in one of two states. Things are either growing or dying. Our own lives are no exception and the only way to ensure that we continue in our growth is to challenge ourselves every day to be better at what we do and to do our best not to let any opportunity slip from our grasp. Successful people did not become successes overnight. They applied themselves every day and little by little they continued to grow and eventually they attained their goal. Anything is possible if we constantly challenge ourselves to be the best every day.

94

YOU ARE ONLY AS GOOD AS YOUR LAST GAME.

Everyone enjoys the sweet taste of success. It is a flavor that we all wish for and it lingers long in our senses. Whether it is a personal victory or a more public success, it feels good to accomplish something, particularly when we are recognized for it. Like almost everything, success is a double-edged sword with both advantages and disadvantages and it is up to each individual to determine what he or she will do with it. We must be ever mindful of the fact that the only constant in life is change itself. Change keeps us all moving and growing and an unwillingness to accept this will keep us fixed in our past. We must be careful not to let the joy of our success keep us stagnant and prevent us from growing as the world around us changes and moves on. The moment of our success can be an anchor that holds us back and keeps us from moving forward, or it can be the catalyst for growth that can be leveraged to propel us to the next success.

Regardless of which path we take, we can be assured that the world around us is going to change and evolve and move on. The memory of our past successes will soon be forgotten by others and we will be recognized only for what we are doing now. High school reunions are classic examples of this effect. Everyone remembers the captain of the football team but if he has not evolved into someone still worthy of that admired status, he will simply be remembered as a has-been who wasted his talent.

The thrill of victory can cause us to lose sight of what is really important. While it is good to take a moment to enjoy the fruits of our hard labors, we must never forget that success presents an opportunity for self-assessment, a chance to reflect on what we did right so that we can build on those choices and use them to become even better. Our past will help to get us in the door but it is our present actions that will keep us in the game. It is great to have stories of experiences that have helped us to grow and develop as a person but it is our actions in the present that define who we are. Our past can be defined by our words and stories while our present is defined by our actions. We recognize people for their past actions because it gives us insight into their potential. From that point on, however, it is only the actions in the present that matter. All glory is fleeting and if we want to continue to grow, then we must put yesterday's victories behind us and decide what we are going to do today. We are judged by how well we play and we are only as good as our last game.

95

PAINT WORD PICTURES.

Although the words we use make up only seven percent of the overall communications process, they are a very powerful seven percent that cannot be ignored or dealt with lightly. Words have the power to influence not only the listener but the speaker as well. As we speak words, we actually solidify our own beliefs and establish our own expectations. As a listener, we form opinions about the speaker and interpret what he is saying based largely upon that opinion. The purpose of communications is to influence the listener and in order to do this, three things must happen.

Number one, we must be heard. As speakers, we have the responsibility to make ourselves heard and this means that we must be interesting enough for someone to listen to us. No one wants to listen to a boring speaker. If our audience is thinking about something else while we are speaking, then they are not listening to us. So, we must be heard.

Number two, we must be understood. Too many speakers think that simply because they put the information out to the audience, it is being understood and interpreted correctly. This may not be the case. There is a lot that takes place between speaking and listening and there is a lot of room for misinterpretation. As the speaker encodes the message and then transmits it to the listener for decoding, the life experiences of the audiences impact how the message gets interpreted or understood. This is why it is never enough to just put out statistics. Statistics can be interpreted in many ways depending upon the life experience one brings to the table. So, being understood is very important.

Number three, we must be remembered. If we do not present the information in a way that enables the listener to remember what was said, we have not done our job as a speaker. We must have a strategy for helping our audience to remember what we are saying. There are many methods for doing this and it is important to understand that it is not the responsibility of the audience to search through a sea of words to find the key points of our presentation. It is the responsibility of the speaker to present the key points in a manner that makes them easy for the audience to recognize what is important and what is not.

All three of these elements must be part of our presentation if we are going to influence our audience and an excellent way to ensure that this happens is to paint word pictures. By presenting information in a way that creates a mental image that can be easily remembered, we cover all three of the elements needed to influence our audience. Word pictures help the audience to relate the information to their personal lives and to see the possibilities of what the speaker is presenting. Once the audience has heard our words and interpreted them in a way that it applies directly to themselves, they will remember that application because it is personal rather than theoretical. Painting word pictures is one way of incorporating the three elements needed to influence our audience.

#96

NOTHING SUCCEEDS LIKE SUCCESS.

The planning process is essential to the accomplishment of any goal. How we structure our path can be an aid or a hindrance to our progress. Our motivation is very often the first casualty in the battle to achieve our goals. Because motivation is so important to our overall success, we must guard it as much as possible. Most people are very susceptible to the feedback they receive in life.

We can set ourselves up for success from the very beginning of a project by developing a plan that has many short-term goals as a part of our overall model. By breaking our goal down into many short-term or intermediate goals, we take what would otherwise seem to be insurmountable and make it manageable for us mentally. You might have heard the saying that "By the yard, life is hard; by the inch, it's a cinch."

The accomplishment of any goal is not the result of one bold action but the product of many smaller actions that culminate in success. For example, if you aspire to be an Olympic runner, you would not just decide to go to the Olympics and run a race. To be selected to run in the Olympics, you would have to run hundreds of races over a period of time and each race would be one more hurdle that you would have to overcome. By understanding that path and making each race a part of an overall plan establishing short-term goals, the runner puts his focus where it needs to be in order to accomplish the task at hand.

This is very important to maintaining our overall motivation. By setting short-term accomplishable goals, we set ourselves up for success and this helps to guard and protect our motivation. With each consecutive success we are energized and further motivated to succeed and to continue to put energy and time into the accomplishment of our goal.

Our attitude has so much to do with how we perceive success and failure. Thomas Edison found success in the failures of those elements that were not suitable to be used as filaments for the light bulb. As he ran each consecutive test, he learned of one more thing that would not work and that was a victory for him. There are many formulas for success and you will have to find the one that works best for you. Small victories go a long way toward keeping us motivated on the long path toward the achievement of our goals; so remember that nothing succeeds like success.

97

USE AN "X" FACTOR.

Product differentiation is a very difficult thing to accomplish in the business world. How to make his company's product different from everyone else's is a source of constant business maneuvering that occupies the mind of every executive. In our fast-paced world there is nothing that is developed that will not be duplicated within a very short period of time and because of this, we must be constantly aware that our competition is nipping at our heels.

Many products are so much alike that the selling of the product has nothing to do with the product itself. For example, Starbucks has made a name for itself by taking the focus off of the coffee and putting it on their friendly and fast service. Although the Starbucks product is coffee, it is too difficult to differentiate the product from coffee that anyone else would sell. The thing that differentiates Starbucks is that they are selling friendly, personalized service, as well as coffee.

So the question is not how good you are, but how important are your differences. How a product is presented is often what makes the difference between a business being successful or unsuccessful.

Audiences are made up of busy people and they are bombarded with information throughout their day. What makes your presentation different? What makes you memorable? What makes your product better than every other product out there? The answer is contained in the question. YOU!! How do you differentiate yourself? It is not about selling your product, it is about selling yourself and the better you do this, the more memorable and influential you will be.

One of the tools that will help you to differentiate yourself is an "X" factor, something that you do or a way of presenting your information that cannot be forgotten by the audience. Speakers must often give presentations in conjunction with other presenters. After the third or fourth speaker, they all start to sound the same to the audience. An "X" factor is something that cannot be easily forgotten. It is designed to help a presenter to stand out as different in the sea of sameness. This should be something that is out of the ordinary and perhaps a little shocking. It can be something that is funny or absurd. It can range from the speaker standing on a table, juggling, doing magic tricks, singing, screaming, or doing a handstand to spraying the audience with a water gun. The action does not have to have any direct application to the presentation itself but it is good if it can be tied in.

If you want your product to be remembered, then you must make yourself memorable. One way to do this is through the use of an "X" factor. When you are preparing a presentation, try to find a way to incorporate an "X" factor to help differentiate yourself from the rest of the pack.

98

SUCCESSFUL PEOPLE ARE WILLING TO DO WHAT UNSUCCESSFUL PEOPLE ARE NOT WILLING TO DO.

Success is measured differently by everyone. One thing is for sure, however, and that is that regardless of what your measurement of success is, it is not easy to achieve. If it were easy then everyone would be successful. Success is the result of a process and of a good plan that helps us to work through that process. People who do find success in life have done so because they are willing to do what it takes. The brass ring in life is available to all who are willing to work for it.

Success has two aspects that must be addressed if we are to achieve our goals. The first is hard work. Hard work is the focus and the discipline to do what needs to be done to accomplish our goal. This is only half of it, however. Being willing to do the hard work is important but the other aspect of success is sacrifice.

While hard work is the physical aspect of success, sacrifice involves the mental battle that must be fought every day. This is the part that most people do not see. We can all look at the product of success and see the hard work that went into it but we don't always see the sacrifice. Success is the result of choice not chance. Life is made up of an infinite number of possible choices and based on the choices we make, we will produce a result that is either good or bad. These choices that we make every day are often subtle but the impact of their nuances is the determining factor in many elements of our life. So much can be learned by observing not only what people choose to do but what they choose not to do as well.

This is why it is so important to constantly analyze our decisions and our subsequent actions to determine if they are in alignment with our goals. Every action we take, regardless of how small, has an impact on our future. With every opportunity we are presented with a choice; to do or not to do. What time we get up, what we wear, do we eat breakfast, do we pray, do we check email and do we exercise are just a small number of the decisions that we make at the start of every day. This is where discipline comes into play.

It is possible to determine the future of a person by the quality of his or her choices. As humans, we are naturally driven toward making our lives comfortable and easy but it is this same human quality that can destroy our future. Successful people are willing to sacrifice comfort and ease for the good of the goal that they seek. Success takes hard work and sacrifice and these take discipline in our daily choices. Successful people are doing what unsuccessful people are not willing to do.

99

USE VISUAL AIDS.

Success is made up of a series of small things that are put together in order to have a synergistic effect, producing a superior result. Success is not the result of a single significant incident that just happens without a series of precursor events that bring it into existence. Many people want to find a single thing that is the key to success. That would make it so easy if it were that simple, if we could say that if you will just do this one thing, you will be successful. Unfortunately, this is not the case. Success is the result of many things brought together in a single moment and each one is important. To ask a person what the single most important thing was that resulted in his success is like asking a doctor what is more important, the heart or the lungs. The truth is that you cannot live without either; they are both essential. So, if we want to be successful we must study all of the associated elements that come together to produce a successful result.

Visual aids are one tool a speaker can use that will aid in the successful delivery of a presentation. Visual aids add an important dimension to a presentation. There are many types of visual aids available to the presenter today and which one you choose will be determined by the resources you have available and the type of presentation you are planning to give. Visual aids help the presenter in many ways. First, they make the presenter appear more knowledgeable on the subject he is discussing since they provide visual proof to support the information being presented.

Visual aids can appeal to the various learning styles of the audience satisfying their need for visual, audio and kinesthetic input. Visual aids also provide the speaker with a partner to work with, offering the presenter an opportunity to be more dynamic and giving him something to talk to. When used properly, visual aids can enhance the flow of the presentation by providing the presenter with an outline to follow. With the use of visual aids, a presenter can demonstrate command of the environment, project more confidence and develop a connection with his audience.

Visual aids are just a small part of the larger, more complex process of influencing an audience. Like any tool, this one has its applications that can be very effective when used properly. It is important to note that visual aids can be equally destructive when they are not utilized correctly. Visual aids are not a replacement for the speaker but are meant to enhance his presentation. Learn the rules for using visual aids and work them into your next presentation.

100

DEVELOP THREE TO FOUR STUMP SPEECHES.

What is a stump speech? A stump speech is a presentation that is short and on point for a topic that is important. It is not a memorized presentation but it is a presentation on a topic that is important to you, the speaker, and is a speech that you have taken the time to develop so that it can be delivered professionally and with the necessary supporting facts. These presentations are not normally on topics that are constantly changing but are generally about the personal philosophy of the individual. Stump speeches are great ways to express your personal values and expectations to your audience. They should not be too long and should take only three to five minutes to deliver. They need to have good content, be well organized and delivered in such a way as to drive the main point.

Stump speeches help us in three ways. One of the first things that a stump speech can do is help us to articulate our personal philosophies. This is very important in the communications process and for a leader, it is essential. We cannot expect people to follow us if we are unable to articulate our own values and expectations.

The next thing a stump speech does for us is that it ensures we never get caught flatfooted. There are many times in a leader's career when he is asked to say a few words or to make an introduction. Having a stump speech in your back pocket that you are ready to present will give you confidence and may even motivate you to look for opportunities to present your stump speech.

Lastly, a well-prepared stump speech will give a speaker credibility with an audience. When people see that a speaker is not afraid to take the opportunity to stand before an audience at only a moment's notice and deliver an excellent presentation, that speaker gains credibility. Every leader wants to be thought of as credible and confident by his audience. Stump speeches are not time-consuming to develop and are great tools to enhance any speaker's image as a leader. Forewarned is forearmed and that is the secret to success in any endeavor. Preparation is key to not being caught off guard and being able to display a calm and confident demeanor in what could otherwise be a stressful situation.

The next time you have a few minutes, think about what you would say to a group of new employees about the policies of your organization or how you would define the culture of your organization. Develop those ideas into three or four stump speeches and be ready for your next opportunity.